WHY WE GOLF

PAUL STALEY

ISBN: 0615482791
ISBN-13: 9780615482798

Chapter 1:   Why Golf?... 1

Chapter 2:   Golf and Evolution 19

Chapter 3:   Fear and Greed.. 31

Chapter 4:   The Nature of the Game 41

Chapter 5:   Bad Golf... 53

Chapter 6:   Things We Say.. 65

Chapter 7:   Golf and Time 77

Chapter 8:   Rules and Handicaps 85

Chapter 9:   Different Ways to Play..................................... 99

The Turn   113

Chapter 10:   Getting Better.. 121

Chapter 11:   The Pre-Shot Routine 141

Chapter 12:   Swing Thoughts 153

Chapter 13:   Golf and the Mind 161

Chapter 14:   Golf and Religion 173

Chapter 15:   Golf and Philosophy 185

Chapter 16:   Golf, Politics and Psychology........................ 197

Chapter 17:   Golf and a Better You 211

Chapter 18:   The Drive Home.. 231

About the Author.. 241

Chapter 1

Why Golf?

So allow me to set the scene. It's not been the best of weeks. You didn't get the sale, or you lost the case, or a deadline got missed. On top of that things aren't so swell on the home front. Your spouse feels you aren't listening, or something along those lines, you're not really sure what was said. But you're sure of one thing: your kids definitely aren't listening.

Ah, but don't worry, all is right in the world, because it's Saturday morning and you're going to tee it up with your buddies. Yeah, a little golf is going to be just what the doctor ordered.

Fast forward to the 5th green. You and your partner are already down 3 and 1. After lashing your drive deep into the trees you ricocheted your recovery shot across the fairway. Fooling yourself into thinking that you still had a chance at par you then proceeded to put your approach shot into the bunker on the right. From there you executed a textbook bunker-to-bunker shot. Since you weren't going to make that mistake again, oh no you're much smarter than that, you decelerated on the next bunker shot and managed to advance the ball only as far as the thick grass right above the trap. From there you stabbed a chip well past the hole. As you wearily bend over to mark your ball, because, hey, now you get to putt, you ask yourself, "Is this how I relax? Why do I play golf anyway?"

Yes, my friends, "Why golf?"

Well, one way to answer this is to consider the alternatives. Every weekend millions of Americans recreate in ways that aren't as inherently annoying. Maybe they're on to something. Let's take a closer look.

First there are all those aerobic forms of exercise: running, walking, biking, swimming, or using one of those contraptions that allow you to do something previously experienced only in disturbing dreams, such as running really hard but getting nowhere or climbing a staircase that never ends. Now these are all really good for you, and the indirect proof of this is the way many people approach these forms of exercise: as something they just want to get out of the way. It all seems much more medicinal than recreational.

But there's a more fundamental problem here. Dogs run for exercise and fun. But they also sign their names by lifting their rear legs. So, when it comes to exercise don't you think we should be aiming a little higher than the preferred form of recreation for creatures that enjoy sniffing hydrants and their best friends' rear ends?

Look, I don't want to sound like I'm making a value judgment here. Maybe you enjoy doing those things. And just so we're being clear with each other, I'm talking about the aerobic activities.

Anyway, I think we should be taking on activities that call upon those uniquely human skills that have evolved over the millennia: abstract decision-making, the use of tools and complaining.

And don't get me started about swimming or boating or kayaking or any of those aquatic activities. If we weren't meant to live in it, we weren't meant to play in it. Yeah, a little of these is fine, but don't get carried away. There's a reason these are popular activities while on vacation: in both cases you're just having fun some place you don't belong.

As for activities that require a vehicle or a special device like a parachute, we need to listen to that guardian of personal safety and oracle of caution and paranoia that lives in all of us, our Inner Jewish Mother: "What are you crazy? You could get hurt. I don't care if all the other kids are doing it. You could get hurt. You're not doing it."

So how about something more social, like hunting and fishing? Like golf they're results oriented and it's not about doing it in less time. After all, golf is a ritualized hunt. You set off in small groups into an expanse of trees and meadows with weapons on your back with the possibility of getting some birdies or even an eagle. And when you're done you hang around in a clubhouse, drink and ask other people what they shot.

But there's an obvious problem. Most of us are city or suburban folks so it's not that easy to hop in the ole pick-up and drive a couple minutes so you can kill something. And besides, I don't know about the rest of you, but I'm a wimp when it comes to killing, gutting and cleaning. I don't even do a good job of cleaning my golf clubs. Besides I prefer things that are a little more abstract, as in competitions based on numbers instead of carcasses. It just feels a bit more civilized.

Of course there are the games of our youth: baseball, football, basketball, hockey, soccer. I've known people to play hockey well into their forties. But most of these people are Canadian so we just have to attribute this to their not knowing any better. For the rest of us, we're better off adopting the Ralph Nader attitude to these age inappropriate activities: unsafe at any speed.

Of course that leaves our country club cousin, tennis. It's a little harder to dismiss, but the sport does have one fatal flaw. Unlike golf there is no handicap system. Your ability to find a "good" game of tennis depends on your finding a player of comparable ability. In golf all you have to do is find somebody who can't play to his handicap.

So, having vanquished the competition, golf stands at the pinnacle of sport. There are, however, the haters out there, the folks who just won't give our sport its due. One example of this is a survey that ESPN published on its website several years ago. The proverbial panel of experts was asked to rate 60 sports on a scale of one to ten for their degree of difficulty in ten categories: endurance, strength, power, speed, agility, flexibility, nerve, durability, hand-eye coordination and analytic aptitude.

You want the bad news? Golf came in 51st. That's out of 60 in case you didn't read the preceding paragraph that closely. If they had been grading on a curve, our game would have flunked. The good news? Golf beat cheerleading by .625 points. Now according to this group the most difficult sport of all was boxing followed by ice hockey, football, basketball and wrestling. I don't have any real issue with those picks, although I'm not so sure about the ranking for wrestling. One ranking that does bother me a great deal however is canoeing, which landed two notches higher than golf. What this says to me is that these experts think that something people do from a kneeling position is more difficult than golf. I don't know, maybe they're right.

What really irks me are what you see when you look more closely at the scores these "experts" assigned. As golfers we'd all concede that our game is not going to score very high on criteria like speed or durability. We'd expect, however, to score pretty high on nerve though. Not with this group. Golf pulled down a big 2.5, and to put that in perspective here are some of the sports that scored higher for nerve: volleyball, Nordic skiing, and, of course, cheerleading and canoeing. Now golf did score on the higher end for hand-eye coordination (6.00; good but not great), but not as high as badminton (7.25). And while we're at it, what's up with giving soccer a 6.5 for hand-eye coordination? I thought you weren't supposed to use your hands.

The one way in which I would concede that this panel was headed in the right direction was their awarding golf its highest score for analytic aptitude, a whopping 6.38 points. Finally a category in which we kicked our new archrival cheerleading's ass (2.25) as well as canoeing (4.25). But my satisfaction with that was tempered when I saw the scores some other sports received for analytic aptitude: field hockey was higher than golf (6.50), as was lacrosse (6.88).

I don't know what conclusions to draw from this. In both field hockey and golf you hit a ball with a stick, the key difference being that the ball is moving in field hockey. But that seems more reactive than analytic. Maybe golf's score in this category would have been higher if we all wore tartan skirts when we played. As for lacrosse's higher score I can only offer the hypothesis that participants have honed their analytic skills because in the back of their minds they are always wondering about a puzzling aspect of their game: How is it that a game developed by one of our poorest communities, Native Americans, has become THE sport for elite private schools?

For all its shortcomings in terms of how this survey of experts treated golf, this survey at least had the veneer of objectivity. One hopes that these experts were not unduly influenced by their personal preferences, although one also has to wonder how any of these experts rated a sport that they had never attempted. But these considerations are clearly not involved in a 2003 survey that asked Americans to name the sports that they most disliked. Here are the top ten, starting with the most detested:

1. Dog fighting
2. Pro wrestling
3. Bull fighting
4. Pro boxing
5. PGA Tour
6. PGA Seniors
7. LPGA
8. NASCAR
9. Major League Soccer
10. ATP Men's tennis

That's pretty select company wouldn't you say? On top of that the three major golf tours took down slots five through seven. If this were the BCS final rankings golf would be in some pretty prestigious bowl games.

But seriously, let's look at the company in which our beloved sport finds itself. It's like the holding cell in some big city jail on a Saturday night. So many questions come to mind. I get the dislike for dog fighting, but is pro wrestling number two because it's violent or because the violence is fake? Is the number four ranking for the ancient sport of boxing, which was rated the most challenging in the ESPN experts survey and therefore, I would hope, worthy of some degree of respect, a sort of baseline for measuring aversion to violence and people find the other three more loathsome because they involve animals or guys in weird outfits? Am I to conclude based on these results that the American public thinks it's worse for a dog to attack another than it is for a guy wearing tight glittery pants to stick a sword in the side of a bull? Or is this really just an affirmation that in general we just prefer dogs to really big cattle with sharp horns?

This list suggests that there are two forms of dislike when it comes to sports: ones that you find distasteful or disgusting and those that you just find boring or tedious. It's fairly obvious that the top four fall in the former category and that everything from golf on down wound up in the top ten because a lot of people find them dull. Which leads me to wonder what happened to bowling in this poll? I have no idea how this survey was conducted but judging from the fact that golf is segmented into its component tours I have to assume that respondents were given a list of sports broadcasts and that golf is actually lucky that the voting was done that way. If you lumped the scores for the three tours together you'd likely have a total high enough to get golf the number one ranking. Imagine playing a sport that is more disliked than dog fighting. Golf is lucky it was a split ticket.

But if we're going to be honest with ourselves (and honesty is one of the virtues instilled by our game isn't it?) we have to accept that golf inspires a particular form of dislike on the part of many non-players. (The periodic hatred for the game that is experienced by those who play it is quite another matter.) The classic putdown of our beloved sport is that "it's nothing more than" or just a "stupid game about" hitting a little ball into a hole.

To which I say, "Yeah? And your point is…?"

Let's start making a list. Hitting a fuzzy ball back and forth over a net until somebody hits it out of bounds or into the net: yes, that definitely sounds like something will lead to a cure for cancer. And all those team sports, are they somehow less existentially ridiculous because you aren't doing them alone? Because I'm not getting the cosmic significance of throwing a ball into a hoop or hitting a puck past a guy who can do the splits when he's on ice skates.

The irony of this is that some of golf's sharpest critics are people who consider themselves sophisticates, the sort of individual that appreciates craftsmanship. Yet the sports that they prefer to golf, namely almost every other one, are often ones in which the competitor who is stronger or faster has an advantage. That seems like taking a step back towards the rest of the animal kingdom. Why not admire a sport in which those more physical characteristics are de-emphasized and instead celebrate a game in which the victor is the one who plans and executes successfully and in doing so conquers his or her inner demons, a game that calls upon a wide variety of skills and that can be played throughout one's life?

And as for the people who dismiss golf because it seems frivolous, well they're probably not that fond of any sport whatsoever. Games are called games because they exist separately from the supposedly meaningful activities of real life. But they are compelling to those who choose to play because within their boundaries they have significance. We compete. We strive to defeat an opponent or increase our mastery. Obviously if you set the stage large enough everything shrivels to insignificance. Why not indulge yourself in a sport that calls on every bit of eye-hand coordination and mental concentration you possess? Why not take up a game that requires you to plan and then execute and not merely react, thus forcing you to confront every bit of fear or anxiety that your mind is capable of producing?

Really. Why not?

Why not golf?

BUILDING UP THE GAME'S STREET CRED

It could be that the experts in the ESPN survey are just channeling a cultural bias against our sport. I've read some articles recently indicating that golf's popularity has, at least temporarily, peaked. Evidently the total number of rounds played has declined in recent years and this decline began before the Great Recession hit.

Let's face it: the sport has always had a bit of an image problem. It doesn't matter that the vast majority of rounds are played at public courses, most people think of the game as something that happens at exclusive country clubs. Many dismiss it as the diversion of old men who have nothing better to do or the setting for shady business deals. Particularly during hard economic times any sport that people think requires too much time and money is not going to get a lot of love. And let's be honest, some phases of golf fashion haven't helped and the whole golf cart thing seriously undermines the contention that you're playing a sport.

Yes, the governing bodies of the game could sponsor more clinics and get more kids involved in the sport. But that's not going to get it done unless we address something else first: our game's lack of street cred.

Think about it. If you're breaking away from the action for a commercial break during an NBA telecast, here comes the hip-hop. Same for the NFL or for the highlight reels from ESPN. I've lost count of how many professional basketball and football players have recorded rap songs. But I do know how many golfers have: zero.

Well, that's over. If you can't beat 'em, join 'em, and it's time we got with it. I'm not saying you have to like it. Do you think the network executives like this stuff? Nah, it's all about marketing, baby.

As for the music, don't worry that's never been much an obstacle for this sort of thing. We'll just get a DJ to sample some nice hook from a song back from pre-digital days when people didn't know any better and wrote melodies and played actual instruments. Then he'll just add some beats and synthesizer effects and we're all set.

For the chorus we need something that is repetitive and can be yelled. "Watch 'em drop, watch 'em drop" is going to be ours. Obviously, at one level, the chorus is referring to putts, and at another to the rapper's opponents. But it could also be heard as having more ominous and violent connotations, which is critical in terms of appealing to our target demographic: white suburban teenagers.

As for the lyrics themselves we are definitely not departing from the basic structure of a rap song. First and foremost there is me, the MC, and there is no limit to the ways in which I am unbelievably wonderful. On the other hand, there is this other person or group of people, always referred to in the second person, who, as my counterpoint, are just as unbelievably pathetic and lame. So as a lyricist I face the dual challenge of describing not only my considerable talents and prowess, but cataloguing "your" deficiencies as well.

The interesting thing is that golf is actually an activity that lends itself to this kind of treatment. We all like to bust on our playing partners from time to time. We just need to turn it up a notch. So let's get the groove goin' while I drop some knowledge.

Pop it and flop it and draw it and fade it
If you see a great shot then you know that I made it.
At the first tee I stroll up and rip her
But you get in more trouble than the Titanic skipper.
You're doing more slicing than a delicatessen
I'm firing at pins like I'm Smith and Wesson.
Your scores are so large you need a mathematician
My ball does more checkups than a pediatrician.

Chorus: Ooooh, yeah, watch 'em drop! Watch 'em drop!
Ohhhh, yeah, watch 'em drop! Watch 'em drop!

Yeah, you got short game, it's your drive off the tee
But I've got Lefty taking lessons from me.
It's always the short grass for me and my Titleist
But you're off in the woods like a wacko survivalist.
Fazio, Dye can't build nothing to faze me
My game has some shots that even amaze me.
You're hackin' up divots like you huntin' for gophers
I'm so fly in my Footjoys they're like Gucci loafers

I bagged more birdies than James Audubon

I'll show you no mercy, my game's always on.
You always hit first except from the tee box
You laggin' three footers like a schoolgirl in kneesox.
My swing is like butter because I'm always relaxin'
Your downswing is faster than an atomic reaction.
It's like Christmas at Hallmark: your card's full of snowmen
Can you keep up with me? The answer is no man.

Chorus

Your game's got more hooks than a Japanese trawler
I'm takin you down to your very last dollar.
My putter is hotter than a sidewalk in August,
But you're blowing up like an angry jihadist.
You want advice on your game, I say look into horseshoes
Get a refund on lessons and all of your club dues.
Will you ever get better? I tell you there's no way.
Take those clubs you're abusing and sell 'em on eBay.

I got shots so great there's no forgettin' 'em
You just stand in your Dockers doin nothin' but wettin 'em.
While I'm bagging birdies you're bookin' doubles
Yeah you swingin' like Freddy: Krueger not Couples.
My shots find the hole like they're guided by lasers
You twitch on the green like your putter's a taser.
I make a divot so my ball has back spin,
You hack out trenches soldiers could live in.

Chorus and fadeout

Before we go into production I want to clarify a couple things about the video. Yes, I will be front and center waving my arms around and wearing a lot of bling, which will consist of bag tags and medallions from places like Winged Foot and Oakmont, because you know I only go to the finest clubs. The chorus will be sung by my posse: D-Dub from Fogtown, Decdog from Limerick and Troyboy. They'll be wearing Titleist and Callaway golf hats and throwback golf shirts.

At the end I will be standing there while my boys yell, "Watch 'em drop, watch 'em drop" over and over again, trying to look as intimidating as possible. Of course I will be surrounded by scantily clad women who will make an appropriately big deal about selecting a club for me or teeing up my ball. There may even be some suggestive massaging of the shaft of my, uh, driver. I could even slip behind one or two of them and show them the proper setup and takeaway. Of course I will be driving a pimped out golf cart with rims and I'll probably wear about five or six different outfits during the course of the video.

GOLF IN CRISIS

In the course of my perfunctory research on the popularity, or lack thereof, of our game I came across an article claiming that over a recent five-year span about four million Americans quit playing golf. As with so much that one can find in that treasure trove of information both erroneous and factual that we call the Internet, there was no substantiation offered for this number. I mean, how do you keep track of something like this? If there had been a nationwide golf club amnesty day like law enforcement agencies have had for owners of outmoded or unlicensed firearms I'm sure I would have seen the photos of people lined up outside fire stations with old style bags filled with Spaulding blades and scuffed Acushnet balls.

When I did a search on why people quit golf I found a survey that touched on this topic but only in an indirect way. The respondents in this case were primarily avid golfers who were asked, among other things, why they thought people quit the game. Now asking people who have little intention of quitting why others decide to abandon the sport is going to provide more insight into the psyche of the avid golfer than it is going to explain the motivations of the former player. In this respect it is a bit of a Rorschach test and in my opinion the results don't disappoint. Here in descending order are the reasons these golfers thought others quit playing:

1. Family obligations
2. Too expensive
3. Takes too long
4. Tried but it was no fun

5. Too difficult

6. Embarrassed by how they played

It's pretty obvious that you can slice this list right in half. The first three are all the ways in which golf affects some of the other people in a golfer's life. I think the technical term for these other people is either 'family member' or 'spouse'. In other words these are the complaints and criticisms that golfers hear from their loved ones and the pre-eminence of these in this survey shows that we devoted golfers may not have changed our behavior in response to these gripes but we have at least internalized them. So we'll call this first half of the list the guilt portion.

But if these first three are a reflection of what golfers hear from others about their games, the second half of the list is all about how golfers themselves feel about the game. It is indeed challenging, is not always fun, and lord knows a golf course can be a veritable mine-field of embarrassing situations. These are all the reasons any of us have thought at times that we might be better off doing something else for recreation and relaxation.

But putting aside my petty skepticism about that particular number of four million quitters in our midst, there is no denying that our game is facing some challenges. Rounds played over the first decade of this century have declined and courses have closed. Certainly economic conditions explain some of these trends. But the fact remains that the anticipated surge in the numbers of golfers that was supposed to occur as the Baby Boomers aged has not really materialized. Several factors explain this, not the least of which is that the premise behind the Boomer Golf Boom was itself flawed. The supposition here was that Boomers were going to follow in the footsteps of their parents, a.k.a the Greatest Generation, and take up the game. But that ignores one of the critical dynamics in human interaction, namely that a significant percentage of people grow up determined to do the exact opposite of their parents and that determination does not go away with the passing of adolescence. Ike golfed, but Ike was our parents. JFK, the President that many Boomers grew up identifying with, also golfed but he kept that very much on the down low and his golfing was almost as big a secret as his philandering.

There is also no ignoring that golf, and all activities that we define as leisure, are fighting a very powerful trend: we are working harder. According to one survey, over the last 20 years working time has increased 15% and leisure time has decreased by 33%. The dirty little secret of the wireless world that has us all hypnotized by our smart phones is that work is no longer confined to the building where your office or cubicle is located. It seeps out into the atmosphere carried on the invisible electromagnetic waves that surround us and it only takes the press of a button and there he is, your boss. We used to go to sleep after bedtime stories about genies that emerged out of lanterns to grant us our wishes. Now we live in a world in which our managers materialize out of small hand-held devices to give us a list of deliverables for tomorrow's staff meeting.

I'd also add into this equation the pernicious role of the kudzu of American family life, soccer. A non-native intruder, its unchecked growth has choked off literally millions of hours of free adult time. In households across the country the soccer schedule is the organizing principle of the weekend. Imagine if time travel had been available in 1962 and you could have transported an average 45-year old male from any typical suburban enclave of that day to a comparable setting in the present. No doubt he would find much to admire and envy, starting with the flat screen high definition TVs and the existence of 24 hour sports coverage on cable. But then visualize explaining to him that you didn't have time to golf that day because your daughter had a soccer game. The unfiltered Chesterfield he was smoking would fall from his lips as his jaw dropped.

There was another argument advanced for an increase in golf's popularity: Tigermania. Supposedly the emergence of a multi-racial golfer as the greatest of his era if not of all-time would encourage wider and greater participation in the game. But this angle overlooked a key element behind Tiger's popularity among non-golfers: the keen satisfaction many people felt when they got to see a man of color kick all those white asses not on a basketball court but on the very courses that had barred minorities for years. Viewed from this perspective Tiger's popularity isn't so much an incentive for viewers to start golfing as it is confirmation of what so many people dislike about the sport: its air of exclusivity and the aura of money and privilege that seems to surround it. Tiger may have been a form of anti-hero to non-golfers long before he became an anti-hero to many golfers in the wake of his sex scandals.

CHAPTER 2

GOLF AND EVOLUTION

Having dismissed most other forms of recreation as too boring, hazardous or messy, that still leaves the challenge of answering the question "Why golf?" in the affirmative.

But I've got good news. I've figured it out. Quite humbly I think I have solved the mystery of why we put up with a game that is so intrinsically annoying.

It begins with the theory, advanced by some evolutionary anthropologists, that we prefer landscapes with meadows and trees because they remind us of the terrain where our ancestors first ventured out of the jungles. Some have argued that the look of a golf course is appealing to us for just that reason.

But that got me to thinking. What if we are drawn to golf not merely for the scenery but because the activity itself is reminiscent of our ancestors' existence? Could it be that golf is, at some level, a ritual re-enactment of the hunter-gatherer's life?

Certainly our experience out on the course provides indirect support for this theory. There's a lot of primitive behavior out there. Dissatisfaction is voiced using the vocabulary of bodily function. People revert to primitive animist notions and yell instructions to small round objects that have no auditory capability. The ability to find small round objects in high grass is highly valued, but knowledge of literature or music is seen as pretty worthless.

But the ways we act on the course are only symptoms of a more fundamental identification we have with this game. For those four or so hours we are re-living the hunter-gatherer existence. And when you think about what that life was like you begin to understand why we are drawn to, and put up with, a sport like golf.

Back then a day at work meant being in the great outdoors with your buddies, but it was still a hard life. If it was easy we would have stayed in the business: "Oh no thanks, I'm not interested in the indoor plumbing and microwave ovens, I'll just rut around in the dirt in my loincloth and see what animals I can kill with these weapons I've made from sticks and palm fronds."

The gig involved a lot of schlepping, a lot of work and a lot of disappointment. But then, every once a while, just enough to make all the effort worthwhile, you struck pay dirt: you bagged that geriatric antelope that couldn't keep up with the rest of the herd. Yeah, the meat was a little tough, but it made for a great family barbeque. And the bad times? They provided the incentive to try different tools or weapons, to tell your friends the same stories you told them last time you were together, or to follow the advice your friends passed along, as in "Thorg, when throw spear, you no shift weight to front foot. All arm no good."

So this is how we spent our days, for a couple million years no less. Every day we set out into an expanse of grassland and trees with the same group of guys and engaged in activity that involved a lot of repetitive motions, the vast majority of which didn't produce the intended result, interspersed with moments of transcendent success. In between spurts of activity there was a lot of time for telling jokes, analyzing what went wrong or thinking about what could have been.

Remind you of anything?

When you look at it this way, you realize that golf is no mere sport. It is the quintessentially human activity. We are descended from people who spent their whole lives dealing with the frustrations and savoring the successes of a quest that is the great-great granddaddy of this noble sport that people dare to call a mere 'game'.

If there were such a thing as a time machine and we could go back to those days I'm sure that we'd observe the same conversations and interactions that take place these days out on the course. There would be the guy who had to tell you about his big success at this spot last time he was out here. There'd be a guy who was always trying out a new spear. Everybody would be yelling at their spears to shift direction while in mid-flight.

Now, one might be inclined to ask, "Wait a minute, if golf is a re-enactment of our primitive ancestors' existence, shouldn't we be better at it?" And the answer to that is the final piece to the puzzle. You see we stopped being hunter-gatherers because actually we really weren't that good at it. Yes, it enabled us to move away from our noisy cousins, the chimps, but that was about it. And, as mentioned above, it was a tough line of work.

At some point we realized that when it came to gathering, pound for pound, squirrels were far more efficient, and as far as hunting was concerned, the big boys in that business saw us as prey, not as competitors. Eventually we heard about this new technology called agriculture and learned to grow our food rather than scavenge for it. We developed symbolic systems for recording things and, most importantly, we learned how to make beer.

Which brings me to a slight detour: my favorite theory of how human civilization started. A professor has argued that beer is the reason that humans stopped roaming and decided to stay put in settled communities. He envisioned the following scenario: there's a camp of hunter-gatherers and they've got the latest storage technology, baskets, and they've left a bunch of these things filled with wild grain around their campground. Well eventually it rains and since they haven't invented lids yet the baskets fill up with water. They let the baskets sit there for a while (I don't know why they let this happen. Maybe the women were away on a spa weekend.) Eventually the weather turns hot and dry and that's when some person, probably a guy, and most likely the dufus who left the baskets out in the first place, gets thirsty and decides to drink the now fermented brew in one of the baskets. And all of a sudden he's the life of the party. He turns his buddies on to his concoction and we're on the road to civilization because beer is good but it's really hard work to lug around baskets filled with mash and water. It makes sense instead to stay close to the beer, to settle in around it as it were. So instead of roaming our species learned to cultivate and build and all because of beer.

The reality that as a species we are better suited for more cerebral activities raises the possibility that people who are actually good at golf are throwbacks. Rather than view them as our superiors, we should see them as merely closer to our pre-civilized selves. Those of us dismissed as hacks or duffers are really just more highly evolved. We've honed our ability to think about the future and worry about the consequences of our actions, all of which are things we're told not to do when in the act of hitting the ball. Have you ever heard how one good player refers to another? He calls him a "good stick." That's real sophisticated. And the golf caps? They're not for protection from the sun. They're for hiding a sloping brow.

In fact I can offer real scientific evidence that supports this. A neuro-radiologist did a study in which he put golfers of various skill levels into a brain-scanning device and asked them to imagine their golf swings. This brain scan measures energy consumption and those areas that light up the most are assumed to be the ones that are consuming the most energy and therefore working the hardest. This scientist found that the brains of the better golfers used less energy than those of the duffers. Now he concluded that this was evidence that as you get more accomplished at a skill the mental energy needed to visualize or execute that action diminishes. The internal programming for that particular action migrates down to the lower level motor maps in the brain and you simply don't have to think about it that much. Well, yeah maybe. There's another possibility: maybe the better golfers' brains simply don't use as much energy for anything because there's not that much going on up there.

So there you have it. I finally have an answer to the question, "Why golf?" It's simple really. We golf because it's in our nature. We just don't know any better.

IF GOLFERS RULED THE WORLD

But viewing golf in this perspective leads us to pose other questions. For example, what if the world, that big expanse of earth and people that we refer to as O.B., operated according to the philosophies and attitudes that we display as golfers? What if the institutions of our daily lives operated according to the Ethos of Golf?

Let's get one thing straight right off the bat. It would not be a world where everybody wears incredibly ugly golf pants. That is so 70's. These days it's pretty monochromatic and muted from the waist down and there's a sort of casual Fridays look from the belt up. I belong to a club in Daly City, California, on the foggy outskirts of San Francisco. Our members look less like Rodney Dangerfield in *Caddyshack* and more like venture capitalists who happen to work in a building where the heating system doesn't work so well. (I should also mention at this point that our club is notable as far as golf garb is concerned as the home course for the owners of Loudmouth Golf, the purveyors of the lurid pants that John Daly has been wearing on tour the past few years. Full disclosure: I own a pair.)

Although some of us fall short of total adherence to the rules of good conduct on the course, I still think that you could safely say that this new world would be one in which people were better behaved. People would know to wait their turn and they would be more likely to clean up after themselves. And, miracle of miracles, even the most talkative would know that there were times when they need to shut up.

As for other ways in which the world would be different, a couple more things come to mind. Chronic deficits would be a thing of the past. How long are you going to play with somebody who doesn't pay his debts? Also it would be a more democratic world in which a single citizen can bring the mightiest to justice. I'm thinking of those instances in which some rule hound sitting in his armchair in LaCrosse, Wisconsin spots an infraction during the telecast of a tournament and starts making phone calls and firing off emails. Before the culprit sets foot in the scorer's tent, the tape has been reviewed, judgment rendered and the penalty, if any, assessed. No special prosecutors and no grand juries required.

It would be more democratic because of the very nature of the game as well. Although we all make a big deal about how we do off the tee that first shot is really not the most important one on most holes. On a par three it's usually the second shot that really counts, on a par four it's the third and on a par five it's the third and fourth. So in other words it's not a matter of what kind of start you get or what advantage you have at the beginning. It comes down to how well you execute and the person who starts off with a big head start doesn't always come out on top.

It's a truism to say that cheaters would not be tolerated. What's more interesting are the modifications a lot of us like to make to the rules and what those changes say about us. I'm not saying that we cheat, only that most of us play a version of the game is less than pure. Why do we amend the rules and what do these changes say about what life would be like if we lived in An Age When Average Golfers Ruled the World?

Generally we don't waste any time before changing the rules. A lot of rounds start with "two off the first." We've only hit the ball once and we're already making things easier for ourselves. The mulligan offends the purist, but viewed another way it's an expression of an equalitarian belief that everybody deserves a good start. There are plenty of difficulties waiting out there and the reload doubles each

player's chances that his round will have, if not an auspicious, at least
an adequate beginning.

Now let's consider how we handle things on the green. The big
boys putt everything out. We concede putts and record scores that
implicitly assume that every one of those two footers were "good."
But why is that? In doing so we deprive ourselves of hearing one of
the sweetest sounds in the universe, the rattle of your ball falling into
the cup. But the flipside of that is the painful ignominy of seeing a
mere 23-inch putt lurch past the hole. So haven't we demonstrated
here that as Average Golfers we place a higher premium on eliminat-
ing suffering than on increasing pleasure? We'll forego that sweet
sound in exchange for avoiding a brief stabbing motion that could
haunt us for the rest of the round. Furthermore, in conceding a putt
we show that our world would be a more merciful one. Every golfer
understands the Biblical injunction to "Judge not, lest ye be judged,"
because you go from judge to plaintiff in the short interval between
the moment when your opponent picks up his ball and your own
slides past the hole.

Viewed from this perspective, a world that followed the Ethos of
Golf would be a more pragmatic place, shaped more by realism than
idealism. In golf, with almost every shot we are confronted with the
gap, or often the chasm, between what we idealize and hope for and
what we actually achieve. In a World According to Golf there would be
none of the extremism born of utopian visions that have led to so much
misery in the past hundred years. Instead we would accept that what we
can accomplish would almost always fall short of what we dream. Yet
we would never give up and we would always enjoy the attempt.

At the same time a World According to Golf would be a tougher
place in certain respects. This isn't so much a comment on the rules

of play as it is an observation based on how we keep score. In this alternative universe there would be only integers, no fractions, no decimal points. There are a lot of implications to living a world of just integers. There is no proportionality: after all the four-inch tap in counts just as much as the 270-yard drive. Life would be measured on a harshly egalitarian scale since all actions would count the same. Quantities that enjoy a unique identity in a world that measures fractional amounts would instead be lumped all together: "Everything under a value of 1.4999, you are all now ones." And compromise would be much more difficult in a world with only whole loaves and no halves. Fractions allow for interaction between numbers, the odd can be divided into the even and vice versa. But there would be no such interplay in this world, and numbers would go about their business, solid and intact, and unconnected to the other numbers around them, much like foursomes on a golf course. In a way it would be like a form of arithmetic apartheid, in which even and odd were allowed only to add and subtract with each other and more intimate operations such as division were kept strictly off limits.

At the same time things assembled of completely different parts would be treated as essentially equivalent because that's what happens in golf: a beautiful drive plus a crisp approach plus an accurate putt is equal to an errant drive plus a satisfactory punch shot plus a miraculous pitch that finds the cup. Two very different animals, but the same identity.

Of course there would be some advantages, such as not needing to use coins to make change, which in turn leads to one of the great ironies in this hypothetical scenario: one of the few places where people would have any use for coins in a World According to Golf would be on the golf course where we would go on marking our places on the green with these relics from an earlier epoch.

But this question of numbers would create an interesting opportunity were Golfers ever to attain their rightful place as Supreme Rulers of the Planet. There's nothing that says we have to have 24 hours in a day. In the new regime this would be changed to the sacred number of 18.

Except for the part about Golfers taking over this isn't as far-fetched as it might seem. The metric system, it should be pointed out, did not originate as a way to confuse American tourists as to the temperature outside their hotel room or the real price that they're paying for gasoline to fill up their rental car. It originated in the French Revolution as a rational scheme of measurement (although the French government did not make the public start using it until the middle of the 19th century). In the same way, after the Golfer Revolution, clocks will be adjusted to have only nine numbers on them. The benefits to society and to golfers would be tremendous.

First off we get rid of these primeval notions of morning and afternoon that really don't divide up that cleanly. What we currently call morning includes the early morning hours that are really part of the night and all those hours after midday are also divided up into different portions of daylight and darkness depending on season and location. In the new regime it's so much cleaner: there's the front nine which takes you to the midpoint of the day and then there's the back nine. "Good morning" would go the way of a lot of what you read in Chaucer, and be replaced by "Good front nine" which as any golfer will tell you is something everybody loves to hear. Learning the basics of another language would also get easier since mastery of counting from one to ten now gets you on the way to being able to greet people.

There would be other advantages as well. Getting heat at home about spending four hours playing a round of golf? Not any more. That's a three-hour round now. See, that was easy. And plus, you get even more time to play because there's no more nine to five. Dude, you're rolling into work a little before seven on the front side and you are out of there and on your way to the course by four on the back side.

So, think about it. Maybe we should put down our range finders and take aim at The Man instead. It might be worth it.

CHAPTER 3

FEAR AND GREED

At this point I think it can be safely said that we've established that golf is not only the greatest game ever, but the quintessential human activity that allows us, nay compels us, to experience the full trajectory of human existence. In a four-hour round we cover the whole arc of progress from flint arrowhead to titanium clubface.

But of course, there's always a catch. Any game that derives from our primeval origins is also going to summon our inner demons as well, the old hobgoblins that made the evolutionary trek with us.

For example, there's an old saying on Wall Street that fear and greed move the markets. If you think about it, this is also true about golf. Now this idea is not exactly like the little devil and little angel that perch on a cartoon character's shoulders when he's wrestling with an ethical dilemma. It's more like two devils and between them they explain so much of what goes wrong on the golf course.

First off, you can put all bad shots into one of two buckets: fear shots and greed shots. The four-footer you left short is a fear shot; the five-footer you gunned past the hole, a greed shot. Anything that involves decelerating is a fear shot. Why did you hit the brakes if you weren't afraid of something? Anything that you pull, from a tee shot to a putt, is a greed shot. You wanted it so badly you jumped on it, didn't you? I'm inclined to think that all bunker shots are fear shots, with the possible exception of the instances when you're short-sided and try to flop it up perfectly and delicately only to leave it in the bunker. That's greed: you wanted the perfect shot didn't you? Well, guess what, you're not that good. You should stick to asking for things you deserve. Anytime you wind up with your weight on your back foot, that's ole devil fear. It's as if your lower body was backing away from the result before you even knew what happened. Anytime you lunge at it, that's greed. Anytime you try to hit an impossible shot like punching a four iron between eight trees, that's pure unadulterated greed. But enough of this inventory of horrors, let's take a closer look at our little friends.

FEAR

Ah fear! How dost thou reveal thyself? Let me count the ways. Fear of playing poorly, fear of looking foolish, fear of hitting it fat, fear of hitting it thin, fear of leaving it in the bunker, fear of losing the match, fear of leaving it short, fear of the first tee, fear of the last putt, the list just goes on and on. But just to make the point painfully obvious, let's look at a phenomenon with which we're all familiar.

We've all experienced having a hole "get inside our heads." You hit a stretch when the particular shot that hole requires becomes impossible to hit. In some cases the problem is chronic and the stretch of time we're talking about is roughly equivalent to your tenure as a golfer. For whatever reason, your age, lack of talent, bizarre swing idiosyncrasies, you simply don't have that shot in your bag. The more annoying instance is when a shot you actually have a chance of hitting starts to elude you. And even worse, this malady is like a turf fungus and migrates from hole to hole over the course of a year. In the spring it could be the approach into number five and the shot into the sixteenth green, but by summer it's the drive on number nine and the shot into the eighteenth green.

Alternatively your nemesis could be not a specific shot but something more situational. In certain respects this is even scarier since it can present itself at any point in the round. One favorite appears to be the approach shot from 30 to 50 yards out. In fact I've had playing partners suggest that this shot deserves its own special chapter. "Write about that one, Staley!" they'll cry out in anguish as another bladed effort skids across the green. I've always suspected that this suggestion has less to do with providing editorial guidance and more to do with the hope that public confession will help exorcise the demons.

When you're having one of these spells, the Chat Room just lights up. In my case, whenever I approach one of these haunted holes or problem shots, there's something going through my head that reads like the Fox News crawl: "...GOLF INSECURITY LEVEL: RED. PAUL STALEY IS ABOUT TO HIT A SHOT THAT HE HAS SHANKED THE LAST TWO TIMES..."

So what do I do when faced with this kind of threat? I do what any red-blooded American does and overreact. I make sure that I come right across the ball with a closed clubface and yank it way left. Now instead of being off in the trees on the right of the fifth fairway, my ball is up in the long fescue grasses above and to the left of the green. I wasn't going to make that same mistake again. Not me. Of course I wound up in an even bigger mess, but still: MISSION ACCOMPLISHED.

In fact the shanks are probably the best, or if you prefer, the worst example of how fear insidiously undermines your ability to play the game properly. Locked in the grip of a shank attack you find yourself unable to do something that you have done thousands of times previously: hit a golf ball and have it go relatively straight instead of squirting off in a deformed version of a golf shot. I came face to face with this conundrum in our member-guest tournament one year. We play the format that has become quite popular for these events: players are grouped in flights according to combined handicap and each team plays the others in their flight in a series of 9-hole matches. You earn a point for winning a hole or the match and half a point for ties. The teams that win their flights then advance to an alternate shot shootout in which teams are eliminated until there are two teams vying for the championship on the last hole.

Although the gallery is modest, and comprised largely of friends and people you know, for the teams that advance this shootout is our only encounter with what "real" tournament golf is like. It is impossible not to be aware that more eyes are watching you swing a club than ever before in your life. Now this particular year my son and I had won our flight and making a decision that I still regret to this day, I decided not to hang out with my buddies and have a beer and a couple laughs. Instead I went down to the range to work on a swing that had become a little too erratic in our last match. In particular I wanted to practice the short iron shot that I was hoping would be my first contribution in the alternate shot competition. Everything was fine until about my tenth swing when it happened: I shanked one. "Oooh, that's not good," I said to myself. "Better erase that from the memory banks as soon as possible." No such luck. I hit another. And then another. And another. Shots squirted off my hosel in rapid succession. Looking over my shoulder I could see a crowd gathering around the tenth tee awaiting the start of the shootout. At this point a full-scale panic set in.

Seeing our club's teaching pro at the other end of the range I ran over and begged for emergency assistance. He proceeded to prescribe the standard remedies, emphasizing the need to swing from the inside. It was all to no avail. Whatever tee or ball he placed as a guide to encourage a proper swing plane just became another object that my club collided with on its way to another pathetic shank. Standing over the ball I felt shanks welling up in me like farts or burps: I could sense them coming and felt powerless to stop them. At one point during his attempts to cure my attack the pro commented that this was one of the funniest things he had ever seen. It is a testament to how much I like him that I have forgiven him for that remark.

I saw my son Adam waving at me to come over to the tee. The shootout was about to begin. I walked over, my body sweaty, my hands clammy. I felt absolutely doomed. I confided in Adam that I was in the midst of the worst case of shanks I'd ever experienced, and although there is no way of proving this, I suspect that my cheery announcement got him so tweaked that he proceeded to put the worst swing of the weekend on his tee shot, launching the ball into an unplayable lie in the trees along the southern side of our driving range. After taking a drop I could still advance the ball only 15 yards, after which Adam ricocheted an iron off a tree leaving us lying four and still 125 yards from a pin that from my angle was tucked between two bunkers. Out of the ten groups left in the competition we were the ones holding everyone up at this point. We were the ones that the whole crowd, competitors and observers alike, looked at and thought to themselves, "There but by the grace of God…"

So there I was, faced with a shot that would have been intimidating even if I hadn't just mutated into a shankapotamus. Going through my pre-shot routine, and addressing the ball as a small gallery watched, knowing that there was absolutely, positively no freaking way I was going to do anything decent was about the worst feeling I've ever had in all my years playing golf. And, sure enough, I came right across the ball sending it arcing to the right like an illustration of a flight path in an in-flight airline magazine. And as an added element of lousiness, it never got more than five inches off the ground. I'll spare you the rest of the story. Suffice it to say we didn't advance past that hole.

Looking back on the event, and on subsequent shank attacks, I realize how the fear of hitting another shank makes the repeat offense just that more likely. At least for me, fear constricts my backswing so that what I think is an adequate shoulder turn doesn't really allow my hands and the club to get back far enough so that I can start my downswing from inside the slot. Combine that with a ballerina-like tendency to get up on my toes and a habit of opening the clubface and you have the perfect recipe for disaster. And fear just pushed me further down that spiral.

Now my travails at that member-guest are an extreme example of how fear can affect your game. A few years ago, though, I came across an article that showed how fear corrupts the performance of even the best in the game. Two professors at the University of Pennsylvania's Wharton School analyzed laser-precise data on more than 1.6 million Tour putts and found that even the best players in the world are fearful enough of making bogey that they make putts for birdie discernibly less often than identical length putts for par. So there is no getting away from it. Guys who make millions of dollars playing this game are also scared of gunning that birdie putt past the hole and setting themselves up for the ignominy of going from birdie opportunity to three-putt bogey. You can dress it up and call it risk aversion, but we're going to call it what it is: fear.

GREED

Fear gets all the press, but greed is right up there as a cause of our problems out there on the course. Like any great duo, they work well in tandem. You can think of them as the treble and bass of your golf game. Fear is the treble, the high-pitched chatter of anxiety, while greed is the bass, the pulse and underlying structure. That irrepressible urge for more was probably an evolutionary advantage when we were showing the other primates that they were living in our world, but it's not such a great thing when we're swinging a golf club. Here are some examples:

Don't deny it because I know you've all done this. This is the scenario. Something is going right. Something is working. Maybe you're more consistent off the tee, or maybe the putts are dropping. So what happens? The next time out you decide that since things are going so well you're going to turn it up just a notch. Since you're so straight off the tee let's see if you can't get another fifteen yards on your drive. Since you're seeing the line so well, let's be more aggressive with those putts.

And we all know how this turns out don't we? You get that extra yardage, right into the trees and rough. And that line you're seeing so well on the greens? Yep, you're getting an excellent read on those four- footers coming back. Now even if you've seen this movie before, you can't stop it from playing on the Not On Demand part of your Mental Golf Cable Package. It's as if at some subatomic level it is so much in our nature to want more that we can't help ourselves. I can go out there and tell myself that I don't want to go back on the rollercoaster and I'm just going to stay inside my game. And yet there I am, coming right over the top as the urge to coax a few more yards out of the ball seems to bubble up from within me.

There's an other variation on this theme and it's the potent little cocktail you get from combining a good round with a couple things you picked up on the Golf Channel or read in *Golf Digest*. You get that tiny burst of confidence and you start thinking that it's time to just add a couple finishing touches. Oh, so Bobby Jones felt the most important move in the golf swing was the hip turn? Well then let's make sure we really emphasize that next time out even though your swing was working just fine last time you took it out for a round. Or maybe it's the super-slow-mo replay of some exceptional player's swing and you think to yourself, "Oh look at what he's doing with his right hand as he comes through the ball. I need to start thinking about that." It's as if we view our golf swings as coming with an option package: "Oh, that's nice but does it come with 15 more yards of distance? Can I get it with the Shot Shaper Package thrown in?" We've banished fear only to clear the stage so that greed can make its own grand entrance.

Another indicator of greed's role in the game is our habit of believing that any round could have been better. There are always the putts that could, or rather should, have dropped. When you broke 90 or 100 the first time I bet it didn't take you long to figure out how that 99 or 89 could have been two strokes lower. In the short time it takes to drive home from my club I can rationalize how almost any round could have been a 79. I'm sure that right after Al Geiberger or David Duval shot their 59's, they could have recalled at least one more birdie putt that could have gone in.

This mental exercise of adjusting one's score to reflect what could have been shows how greed seduces us into exploiting a fundamental inaccuracy about scoring in golf. Assigning a specific number to a round conveys a sense of precise measurement of performance that's really misleading. Obviously how you score on any given day depends primarily on the quality of your game. The better you are the lower the absolute number and the narrower the range of outcomes. Yes, the 86 you shot on Saturday was better than the 88 on Sunday. But both days you were performing within the same range and it was only random events that determined the difference in outcomes. Maybe the greens were a little bumpier on Sunday, or maybe Saturday the ricochet went into the fairway instead of into the woods.

Every time your ball leaves the clubface you've launched it into a natural world where all sorts of random stuff happens. We all understand that. Where greed kicks in is that we like to start with our score and work down from there. The blind squirrel events like the snaking 35-footer that found the hole on number seven is simply something we had coming to us and the putt on number fourteen that was just outside the leather and then stayed just outside the hole was something that was taken from us. It's as if we believe that all the suffering we've endured entitles us to some payback.

(Yes, there are players who say things such as "It could have been much worse" after a round. But who likes rational self-effacing people anyway? And besides, have you noticed that nine times out of ten that comment is just a way of prefacing a statement to the effect that "at least I was putting well." Hey, I don't remember asking how you were putting.)

Finally, for those of you who may doubt the role of greed in the game, let me pose the following question: What do we call a short putt that is conceded by your opponents? That's right, a gimme. Gimme, gimme, gimme. I rest my case.

CHAPTER 4

THE NATURE OF THE GAME

For all our whining and bitching about it, the inherent difficulty of golf is supposed to be one of the reasons for the game's addictive appeal. If it were easy we'd eventually all get bored and quit. I will grant that this is basically true, but haven't we all felt at times that the game goes a little overboard in terms of making that point? It's not as if we'd all get bored and take up hang-gliding if the cups were cut just a little bit bigger.

So why is the game so difficult? As we discussed in the last chapter, golf is an arena in which our primal emotions get to bat us around. But to find the real answer you have to get beyond the unnatural act that is the golf swing and the pastoral sadism practiced by most golf course designers. The source of golf's difficulty lies in the counterintuitive nature of the game.

Most of us were told about the paradoxes of the game when we were introduced to it. If you want the ball to go up, hit down on it. If you want to hit it far, swing easy. The problem is that deep down inside parts of us never accept these bits of insight about the game, clinging instead to the old core beliefs about how the world works. I'm talking about the part of your mind that knows that if you want to get something up in the air you have to lift it, and if an object needs to travel a farther distance you have to apply more force to it. And so, we go on skulling our pitch shots and over-swinging on the tees of long par fours. If a three-iron makes the ball go farther than an eight-iron that's because you swing it harder, right? I mean that's obvious, isn't it?

Yet saying that the game is counterintuitive understates it. Counterintuitive makes it sound as if the game were in opposition to only one part of us, a part which, by the way, women are supposed to have more of than men, when in actuality the game is counter to every fiber in our being. If you're behind in a foot race, you run faster. If you're facing a deadline at work, you just work harder, or if you're a member of a private golf club, you have other people work harder. The point remains the same: a greater challenge equals a greater effort. But try and apply this principle of greater exertion out on the golf course and you are bound to screw up. Faced with the necessity of executing a great shot you are supposed to relax and swing easy. That can feel about as logical as a manager telling a prizefighter who's returned to his corner after getting shellacked in yet another round that the key to turning the fight around is knowing that the other guy is ticklish.

An unfortunately all too common situation illustrates how golf is counter to our natures. How many times have you missed the putt or put your drive in the woods, and then said to yourself, or your partners, "I should have stepped away"? But you didn't, did you? Instead you told yourself that despite your misgivings you were going to buckle down and see this thing through. Isn't this how you solve all those more significant issues like stuff at work or at home? So why shouldn't you apply the same approach to something as trivial as hitting a golf ball? Furthermore, backing away from a challenge wasn't how you earned the money to join a private club, and even if you inherited the dough, somebody in your family tree had guts. So if Grandpa was tough enough to build a business from scratch, then you're going to hang in there on this drive even if it feels like you're lined up sideways to the ball.

For me another indicator of golf's contrariness is my body's inability to understand and follow apparently simple pieces of golf advice. My mind can say things like "Swing easy," or "Relax" and something completely wrong happens. It's as if I were talking to the parts of the enterprise that are actually going to be doing the work but my Spanish wasn't good enough. If I tell myself to swing easy parts of me such as my legs will interpret that to mean that they can just sit this one out. It's as if they were saying in response, "Swing easy? No problem. We'll just let the arms do all the work this time." And the advice to relax can also get lost in translation. When I'm told to relax I tend to think about getting comfortable, and what's more comfortable than a habit, particularly a bad one? In fact, don't most of us have at least one or two bad habits that we use to relax? But I guess that's another topic. Anyway, the relaxed me will often go back to one of my trusty old buddies, like coming over the top.

So next time you're about to call yourself an idiot as you head off into the woods in search of your ball for what seems like the millionth time, stop yourself. It's the game that's back asswards. Your assumptions about how the world works are fundamentally accurate. Just not on the golf course.

Your Brain on Golf

So let's review what we've discussed so far. Golf dominates all other sports, which suck in comparison. Case closed. But it's really really hard because not only does it prey on our fears and wants, but the precepts of good play just don't jibe with the rest of our lives. Is the problem perhaps in the way our brains are designed?

As golfers we're supposed to take consolation in the observation that our chosen form of recreation is a particularly difficult game. "It's a hard game," we'll say to ourselves as we rake out one greenside bunker before trudging across the green to hit out of the sand trap on the other side. "Hard game," a sympathetic partner will say softly as we tap in our fourth putt.

True as it may be, I don't think this statement goes far enough. It's not merely a matter of the game being difficult. We simply weren't meant to play it. By this I mean something a little more insightful than the notion that if humans were meant to play golf we'd have thin metallic arms and grooves on the palms of our hands. (But just to stay with that thought, it's clear that we took an evolutionary wrong turn millions of years ago. Because if we were meant to play golf without using equipment then the ideal build would be somebody built low to the ground with long arms, in other words, somebody who resembles a chimpanzee. My personal theory is that the grasses on the African savannah were just too high for the game. You could hit it straight as an arrow and your ball was still going to get lost. In this setting the ability to hit a golf ball with one's hand wouldn't have offered any advantage in the struggle for survival. Now if we had evolved from primates originating in Scotland....)

No, the problem is all in our heads. We are just not wired properly for the game. I've done extensive research on this question, which means that I've read an article in *Time* magazine about the brain and googled a couple unfamiliar words and terms. So I don't think there can be any question about the validity of my conclusions.

There are three main parts to the brain and there are all sorts of Latinate medical names for the subcomponents. We're not going to get too involved with these since the only important thing we as golfers need to know about the brain is that with its three part structure it is essentially like a Pro V1. That's all you have to know.

In a very simplified way this is what happens when you try to get up and down from one of the bunkers on a difficult par-three. The decision starts in the prefrontal cortex. This is the rational part of the brain, the part that can compute the 18 hole score of a 25 handicapper without the use of a calculator, or that can figure out who owes what in a two-ball game that also includes three indies and $1 junk in the time it takes to walk from the eighteenth green to the proshop. Now as you start the actual execution of the shot, the message about aligning your shoulders with the slope and hitting behind the ball gets routed through the limbic system on its way to the motor cortex which controls the muscles. It's this trip through the limbic system that gums up the works.

I used to think that the problem was that my instructions about golf shots had the same effect on my brain that an ice cream truck has on a neighborhood full of children. The thought starts moving through my head and before I know it all these little creatures are swarming around asking for things like "Give me something chunky," or "Make it a fat scoop!" Or, if you prefer a more quasi-scientific analogy, I thought that my interior golf instructions created a field of static electricity that attracted all sorts of golf particles like the shankatron and the chunkoid. I thought the problem was that my neurotic impulses were attaching themselves to instructions that were following a fairly straightforward circuit.

Not so! The problem is this detour through the limbic system, which is a veritable food court of human emotions. It is usually described as the area of the brain associated with emotions such as fear, anxiety, elation and satisfaction. That's a nice mixed bag. Now why would my nerve centers for satisfaction be in the same neighborhood as those associated with fear? Isn't that a little like putting a chemical plant next to an elementary school? Who's doing the zoning here?

So, it's no wonder that things don't turn out the way I visualized it when I was pretending to go through a pre-shot routine. My innocent little request to hit a simple seven iron gets routed through a place where all these bad actors are hanging out. Using a hub may work for airlines, but not for golfers.

It turns out that the limbic system is one of the oldest parts of the human brain and can be found in fish, amphibians and reptiles. So let me net that out for you. This means that when we're trying to hit out of a downhill lie in a greenside bunker, we're using a hard drive that was designed for a frog. But the relationship between brain design and the game of golf makes sense in at least one respect. It turns out that the limbic system is closely associated with the olfactory lobes. Why have it any other way? Of course, the part of the brain that governs my golf game ought to be connected to my sense of smell.

POSTSCRIPT

If you want something that qualifies as hard scientific evidence that the average Joe isn't wired properly for this game, consider the following study that was conducted on that rare and abnormal class of human, the expert golfer. Evidently the University of Zurich found that really good golfers have a higher volume of the gray colored closely packed neuron cell clusters that are known to be involved with muscle control. On the surface this finding would appear to belong with other major scientific breakthroughs like the report that found the good basketball players tend to be taller. However it does show that there are brains that are better suited for the game.

But of course the discussion couldn't stop there. It's not all genetic destiny and fate. Putting aside my snarky dismissal of the pioneering research findings at the University of Zurich, studies of the human brain reveal that our minds are far from hard-wired. I don't think it possible for anybody in the past few years to have read an article or heard a feature story on dieting or any other self-improvement plan without coming across the concept of brain plasticity. This is the notion that the brain changes with anything we do or think. New connections are made and thus the path to a slimmer you or better mastery of some skill is literally along the pathways that practicing this new habit forms in your brain. The challenge is that you also have a well-worn and very familiar set of connections that are your old way of doing things and our minds are fond of just traipsing along a set of connections that are quite literally the path of least resistance. The beauty of it is that we can change all that.

REALITY: YOUR REAL OPPONENT

But perhaps the challenges of golf stem from causes even more fundamental than the fact that our brains are like one of those houses that started out as a cottage and then had a bunch of additions tacked on. Maybe the problems originate in the very nature of reality.

Let's start with what I'll call an "excuse theory," the application of a scientific theorem to explain and therefore rationalize lousy performance. I know it's rather obvious and redundant to bring this up since I know that most of you are always discussing it with your playing partners, but one of my personal favorites in this regard is Heisenberg's Uncertainty Principle. This refers to an annoying characteristic of sub-atomic particles, specifically the impossibility of making a simultaneous accurate measurement of both their speed and position. You can measure one, but in doing so you mess up the measurement of the other. As a result you can know speed but not position, or vice versa. Now, doesn't that dilemma sound familiar? Of course: it's just like putting. You've got speed and you've got line, and how often do you get them both right? Einstein may have famously remarked that he didn't believe that God played dice with the universe, but I know He does with my putts!

In fact, I can actually cite scientific evidence in support of this. In his book, "Putt Like the Pros", Dave Pelz describes an experiment in which he uses a specially designed ramp as a "robotic putter." He could line the thing up exactly and he could adjust the height of the ramp in order to have just the right amount of speed for a ten-foot putt. The results were, depending on your perspective, either immensely comforting or really discouraging. When Pelz used the "True Roller" on the greens of Bethesda Country Club only 54% of the putts rolled in. Even on the Monday afternoon perfection of the exquisitely groomed greens of Columbia Country Club, 'only' 84% of them went in.

The comforting interpretation is that if a robot misses half of these, then how can you be expected to do any better, or even as well. You should be grateful you sink any of yours. The half empty take on it? If the robot, who by the way has no money on the line, can only make five out of six attempts when conditions are absolutely perfect, then you know you're playing a game where the odds are stacked against you from the start and you can spare us the histrionics next time one of your ten-footers doesn't drop.

While we're using the principles of physics to explain the difficulties of the game, let's drag out that old favorite, the Second Law of Thermodynamics. This states that "the entropy of the universe tends to a maximum." Things progress, in a manner of speaking, from a state of relative order to one of disorder. In other words, things fall apart. Now, how many of your frustrations as a golfer does this explain? Like, all of them, maybe? Let's make a list: the atrocious back nine that you tack on to a beautiful front, the double bogey that you deftly craft out of the longest drive of the group, the errant drive immediately after a birdie, the three jack after getting on in regulation, that wonderful sensation of having the thing that you were doing well on Saturday completely abandon you on Sunday.

I think that the Second Law also explains why tips seem to have a useful life of one, maybe two rounds. Somebody mentions something to you, and for a while this bit of advice provides a new orientation. You think about "It", whatever "It" is, and for a while things click. But meanwhile everything else that's involved in hitting a golf ball starts sliding and drifting all over the place, and after a while "It" is no match for the increasing disorder in your swing. Pretty soon you're looking for another tip.

This is why I've come to view tips as similar to a brand new toy in the hands of a toddler. It starts out all shiny and new. It looks great and it works fine but then in short order it's all covered in drool and fingerprints and stops doing the few simple things it was designed to do.

Next, let's revisit evolution and it's relevance to the game of golf. I like to think of myself as having a decent short game. It's not as if I'm going to be appearing in any instructional photo spreads in *Golf Digest*, but I can pull off the shots every now and then. But then one day it occurred to me that my skills around the green were developed out of necessity because my approach shots are so inconsistent. This notion that I had adapted to difficult circumstances brought to mind the movie *March of the Penguins*. The film was a box office success because people saw it as a testament to love and the will to survive in the face of incredible adversity. But other viewers were less impressed, seeing instead only a documentary about an existence that sucks big time.

Don't get me wrong, I liked the movie. But I also think that if you sat a bunch of penguins down and showed them footage of how other birds live, they would see themselves as a bunch of fat losers who wound up living in the worst neighborhood on the planet. When they could see that their distant relatives can actually fly, the ability to scoot across the ice on their bellies wouldn't feel so impressive. At that moment I think the penguins would realize how they got screwed and, if given the opportunity, would vote unanimously for a rewind of the evolutionary clock.

So what's my point? My point is that a good short game is helpful and at times impressive, but like the ability to balance an egg on one's feet during an Antarctic winter, something that is developed out of necessity, and not always out of choice. In this way evolution explains the peculiar and sometimes lopsided ways in which our games develop. Yeah, I know, there are players who have the complete game. But you know what, evolutionary theory has a term for them as well: mutants.

CHAPTER 5

BAD GOLF

Understanding the origins of Bad Golf is a challenge. Now, if we're really going to be scientific about this we have to consider a number of hypotheses. One winter during flu season it occurred to me that bad golf might be a disease. If you accept that premise then the logical first question is whether it's bacterial or viral. That's an easy one. On any given day, the golf courses of America are full of people on antibiotics and the drugs are clearly not doing them a bit of good. It's definitely viral.

Now if you think that this notion of a Bad Golf Virus, or BGV, is just another far-fetched metaphor, consider the following. Ever notice how the good players tend to play together? You didn't think it was because they actually like each other, did you? No, they're smart students of the game. They've studied the research and they know about the virus. They don't talk about it because they don't want to alarm the general population. Basically it's all about reducing their chances of exposure by keeping the rest of us in quarantine. Playing with us would be like sleeping with a bunch of Cambodian chickens.

So what do we know about the BGV? First, it's not so lethal that it kills the host. If it were, we'd all just quit the game. Instead it's devious and therefore far more effective. Rather than making you put your clubs up for sale on eBay, it makes you think that you need newer and better equipment as well as lessons and expensive trips to golf courses in exotic locations. Instead of considering other forms of recreation, you find yourself wanting to play more in the belief that you'll get better, when in actuality you're only giving the BGV more opportunities to turn your golf synapses into mush.

Second, centuries of evolution have created a virus that appears to "know" the game of golf. It starts with the mental process of your pre-shot routine, then it moves on to the swing itself and finally it attacks a victim's entire personality structure. Here are some of the warning signs of exposure to BGV.

One of the first symptoms of BGV is a feeling of disorientation. When playing well, a golfer can visualize very distinctly the shot he wants to make. When infected with BGV the signals don't come in clearly anymore. We often say that somebody playing well is "dialed in." Well, this is quite the opposite. Instead of seeing the shot as if it were in Hi-Def Slo-Mo, it's more like trying to get a clear picture on an old Magnavox with a coat hanger for an antenna. This is how the BGV begins its sinister work, by attacking the ability to carry out the first step of the pre-shot routine, visualization of the shot.

A healthy golfer proceeds next to step two: committing to the shot. A golfer afflicted with BGV is unable to commit. His golf inner voice no longer sounds suave and cool like Sean Connery, but more like Woody Allen on diet pills. With the pre-shot routine totally short-circuited, the BGV moves on to the swing itself.

A video recorder provides a great way of illustrating what a golfer suffering from BGV looks like. Record a professional tournament and then watch it on fast-forward. See how the players look like Charlie Chaplin when they're walking down the fairway. Funny looking, aren't they? But observe what they look like when they swing the club. They look just like we do when we're playing poorly. Zoom, zoom, zoom. That's the work of the BGV.

With his or her tempo destroyed an infected player's condition can rapidly deteriorate. Now the disease starts to attack the player's ego structure. At this stage you should be on the lookout for expressions of exasperation in which the infected player apparently no longer sees himself as a whole human being, but rather as only a body part. A popular choice is to refer to oneself as what we could politely call the primary exit door for the facility. As the round progresses an infected player will start saying things that indicate that he has stopped seeing himself as evenly partially human and instead as an inanimate object, often a vehicle with mechanical problems such as improperly attached wheels.

But it is during the last few holes of the round that the true nature of the BGV reveals itself. As he approaches the clubhouse an infected player will say things such as "It was just one of those days," indicating that, although he should, in some way he no longer holds himself totally responsible for his poor performance and hopes instead that things will be better next time. Thus you can see how the BGV, rather than destroying the patient once and for all, pulls back, biding its time and waiting for the next opportunity to break out.

So what's a golfer to do? Development of a vaccine is decades away, if it happens at all. In the meantime, the best we can hope for is that brief exposures to small amounts of BGV will help us develop immunity. And above all else, we should be kind to the afflicted because it's the right thing to do, and who knows, you could be next.

BAD SHOTS

In certain ways it would be great if there were something like the BGV. There would be an external cause for our problems. It would be like communism in the fifties: we could just blame everything on it.

But the question still remains: where do all the bad shots come from? Sometimes they pop up out of nowhere, like a jack-in- the-box. The round's going along fine; nothing that would indicate that you should think about qualifying for the Senior Tour, but certainly satisfactory given the standards of your game. And then–whammo!!– you're retrieving a dishcloth-sized divot that not only outweighs your golf ball but has traveled farther as well. Other times they come in swarms, erupting like bats out of a cave in some old horror movie, squealing and thirsty for blood, mainly yours.

After all, the elimination of the awful shot is the real path to improved scores. Our challenge isn't so much playing our best golf as avoiding our worst. A Columbia University professor's analysis of over 43,000 shots from a representative cross section of golfers found that a golfer posting an average score of 105 has four times as many awful shots (8.1 per round) as a low-handicap player who shoots an average round of 80 (2.1). Those are the ones that cost you.

Since there most likely isn't anything like the BGV, we're left with all the usual instructional B.S. about poor shots being the result of things we're doing wrong. But if there isn't a viral cause wouldn't you also accept a more supernatural explanation, or at least one where you weren't considered totally responsible? This is a hectic age in which we live, and most of us are constantly juggling work, family and friends. Wouldn't it be nice to be cut some slack when it came to your golf game? It's unfortunate in a way that the concept of being possessed by evil spirits is so much out of favor these days.

If we lived in a pagan polytheistic world like ancient Rome we might have little altars around the course where we could make an offering to banish the bad spirits or placate the gods. You could offer up something such as a small animal, or cash is always good, to a god like Mercury. Feeling bad about that shanked approach shot on number five? Oh well, another pigeon bites the dust. Instructors wouldn't give lessons anymore. They'd just sit around in togas looking at bird entrails and telling us what we could expect to shoot that day.

We could take our abdication of responsibility even further by believing that the problems were caused by equipment that was possessed by demons. Every full moon there would be a ritual destruction of drivers, irons and putters that had fallen into the clutches of the dark side. Certainly the folks at Callaway and Titleist would see the merits of this approach.

But, for better or for worse, we live in the modern, supposedly more rational world, one in which we are kinder to animals and harder on ourselves. Harry Truman had that famous sign on his desk that said, "The buck stops here." As golfers we have to look in the mirror and say, "The double bogies start here."

And indeed the elimination of those Big Numbers is the key to a better game. Or as stated above, improvement is not so much the result of playing better as it is a matter of avoiding playing our worst. According to the exhaustive statistical research done by the aforementioned Columbia University professor, the typical golfer who shoots in the 90's loses about six strokes to awful or doubly-awful shots, the latter being the ones that bring the stroke and distance penalty into play. And despite the age-old advice that a better short game is the key to lower scores, the really bad shots are more than twice as likely to happen in the long game. Stubbing a chip or jerking a putt is certainly aggravating and adds yet another stroke to your score, but the big damage comes when you have a weapon in your hand that can really propel your ball into the nether world of water or O.B. or the woods. That's when the addition really kicks in.

THE TIMELESSNESS OF GOLF

The topic of bad shots raises another, and possibly eternal question, "How is it that I can lose my swing but I can't forget how to hit a bad shot?"

Let's break this one down into its components. First, there's the issue of losing your swing. Listen, like it or not, they're all your swings. The grotesque effort that put the ball into the driving range when you were teeing off on number ten is as much yours as the swing that put it right next to the pin on number three. Of course when we talk about losing our swing we're talking about the swing that produces good results and not the other ones in our portfolio.

And misplacing it, or if you prefer a more passive role in the debacle, having it abandon you, is a very frustrating experience.

During the 2005 AMEX Championship at Harding Park in San Francisco I heard one of the commentators announce, "Tiger has lost his swing." If that didn't scare you, you weren't paying attention because if he can lose it there's no hope for the rest of us. Of course Tiger found his swing two holes later, which only goes to prove that proportionality is one of the governing principles of the world since the rest of us can go two months before finding ours again. That assumes that we would want to find ours, since the thought of us looking for these swings reminds me of that Rodney Dangerfield joke about getting lost as a kid and asking a policeman where his parents could be, to which the cop responded, "Who knows, there are so many places they could hide."

But if your good swing can waft away like smoke, why are bad shots like something you can't get off your cleats? Doesn't it drive you crazy that skulling a chip is like riding a bike: you never forget how. And why is this?

I think the answer lies in what I call the Timelessness of Golf. Usually that phrase is used to describe places like St. Andrews or conversations that involve a lot of scotch, wood paneled rooms and debates about Hogan at Carnoustie or Nicklaus and Watson at Turnberry. But I'm thinking of something more psychological, and definitely more sinister. It's more a case of how your past will be your future because it's right there with you in the present. I think I probably need to explain myself.

Get out an old photo album and leaf through it. Ah, look, there's your fat little self at your third birthday party, and much farther on there's a wedding picture. Man, where did you get that suit? Was that a prank by your best man? And is that a helmet, or is that really your hair? Anyway, the point is that although you have the same name and Social Security number as the person in those photos, you are in many respects a different person. In fact every cell in your body has been replaced several times over since those photos were taken. (At this point I feel the need to point out that this cell replacement process does not apply to brain cells. The ones you killed at the bachelor party aren't coming back.)

But, of course, your golf self is another thing entirely. Think instead of one of those sets of Russian dolls, the ones that nest inside of each other. The biggest one, the one on the outside as it were, that's your current golf self. Take off the top and there's another one inside. That's you before you took those lessons last year. And so it goes until you get to the last, smallest doll. That's you as the beginner, the one who always looked up too early or swung too hard, and he's still there with you. Isn't that wonderful? This is what I mean by the Timelessness of Golf. We carry around all our previous golf selves inside us.

In a way it's the exact opposite of that scene in every cornball sports movie, the one that takes place shortly before the montage of training scenes, in which the manager or coach says to the kid, "Kid, listen to me pal. Ya gotta look inside yourself, deep inside, ya hear me? There's a champ inside you and he's just waiting to get out. But you gotta bring him out, ya hear me?" I don't know about you but I'm pretty sure my inner champ decided he had a better shot in some other body and just took off. But that high strung little kid who chunked up his first divots at Palo Alto Muni? Oh, he's still there, just waiting for another chance to show what he can do.

Postscript: I had something that qualifies as partial confirmation of this theory of the Timelessness of Golf during my club's home and home matches against Stanford several years ago. I had the pleasure of playing against a guy I had gone to high school with down in Palo Alto. At some point during the match I commented, only partly facetiously, that I felt that I had a hard time hitting good iron shots because I first learned the game on the baked bay mud fairways of Palo Alto Muni. I don't know if conditions have improved since then, but back in the day, the course was basically a thin veneer of grass laid over an expanse of dried mud that had a hardness that would qualify it as a building material in most Third World countries. Hit it just a little fat, and you looked like Fred Flintstone when he went out to cut down trees in the Petrified Forest. Imagine how gratified I felt when my old friend agreed and said that he had the same problem. He then proceeded to hit his approach stiff on sixteen and won the hole. That's what I meant by partial confirmation.

UP AND DOWN

You have to admit that the idea of a bad golf virus or attributing a bad round to supernatural causes is certainly appealing. It's not us, or the game, it's these teeny little microbe things or evil spirits that get us all screwed up. But unfortunately these hypotheses have to be discarded. We're back once again to considering the nature of the game.

Let's start with a snippet of conversation between two golfers:

Golfer A: "Hey, how's it going? How's your game?"

Golfer B: "Oh, you know how it is. You think you have it figured out and then...." (At this point Golfer B's voice trails off, he starts shaking his head and his eyes get that 1000-yard stare in them.)

Golfer A: (nodding sympathetically) "Yeah, I know what you mean."

We've all been there. For some reason we've devoted ourselves to a game that can be described in slightly automotive terms: goes from 79 to 91 in one round. We think we're getting better and then, whamo, we're thrown backwards.

At times our games feel like one of those math problems we had in elementary school: "A frog falls into a well. The first day the frog climbs up five feet only to fall back four feet that night. The next day the frog climbs three feet but then falls four feet again. How long before the frog starves to death?"

There is something vaguely fundamentalist about it: "Yea, verily I say unto you, see how the proud are humbled. Their golf balls are scattered into the trees and high grass and their wallets emptied because they spoke unto themselves, saying 'Hey I think I've got it figured out.'"

Yes, with instruction and practice we can get better, but the course of that improvement can look like one of those graphs of the stock market over time. On any given day one of our rounds could be described as follows: "Staley Golf closed down $15, as the ten-handicapper failed to break 90. It was another disappointing earnings report and analysts cited continued weakness in the short game, particularly from the bunkers. Potential partners have expressed a reluctance to team with Staley in future games pending a new index report from the NCGA at the beginning of next month."

So what's the deal? Why are our results so erratic? One popular explanation is that we are playing an unforgiving game. Or so we like to say to ourselves after recording our third consecutive double bogey.

But I've decided that's not exactly accurate. And besides, there's something sort of whiny about saying that the game isn't fair or is unforgiving. What did you expect? It's occurred to me that if we violated the rules of good performance and good conduct as consistently in that alternative existence we call day to day life as we do on the golf course we all would have been disowned, divorced, indicted, convicted and locked away years ago.

But there we are, back out there every weekend with our rap sheet of offenses: the open clubface at impact, the off-kilter swing plane, the head bob that's supposed to lift the ball in the air on a pitch shot, the head jerk on short putts. The game doesn't kick us out of the house, or hand us a pink slip. You can keep showing up. The game doesn't care.

And that is the essence of it. It isn't that the game is unforgiving. It's just indifferent. Golf is like a blackjack dealer in Reno at 3am.: "Sure, you wanna play? Fine with me, that's why I'm here." What we perceive as unforgiving is merely a game that proceeds on autopilot because each individual outcome is dictated by inflexible rules. Just as the casino is an arena in which the laws of probability administer reward and penalty, events on the golf course must obey a different set of laws, those of physics. And in both cases, disaster awaits whenever wishful thinking tries to ignore immutable law.

At the risk of overly generalizing, at the physical level our misfortunes on the course stem from two causes: first, the magnification of small differentials in angle and vector when things are happening at high speed ("Want to hit a provisional?"), and second, the increasing role of the random when things start to slow down ("Oh, man, I thought that putt was going in!"). Or to give this description some brand identity, the formulas kick in at those brief instances when

TaylorMade meets Titleist, and Titleist meets FootJoy imprint near the hole. It's at once frustrating and fascinating to see how our little game encompasses both Newtonian and modern physics.

But of course these white balls don't just show up at the first tee and propel themselves into the trees to the left. We need somebody to get things going and this, for better or worse, is where we come in. Rules may limit the number of clubs we're allowed to carry, but unfortunately there is no limit on how much we can lug around in our heads.

So, on the one hand we have a game that merely does what it does, and on the other, a collection of players who do what they do and get ticked off about it. When we play golf we are actually standing on the fault line where psychology meets physics, and that is why our games have that erratic quality to them. Things always get shaky when two different realms bump up against each other.

In this respect golf is no different than other intersections in human existence. For example, how about religion and politics? Now there's a recipe for smooth sailing. The stock market? That's the roller coaster ride at the intersection of psychology and economics. Or if you prefer an example closer to home, how about that area of friction where biology rubs up against social norms, a.k.a. adolescence. Yeah, that's real serene.

Yes, our erratic performance across the spectrum of intervals (from shot to shot, round to round and month to month) can be extremely exasperating. But really, how could it be any different?

CHAPTER 6

THINGS WE SAY

So how do we deal with such a difficult game? One place to start is what we say out on the course. I'm not talking about the banter about sports or the past week's events. I'm more interested in what we say to the golf ball, or to ourselves, once we've launched it in motion. It's really some crazy stuff.

In a certain sense these are the moments that most reveal how we feel about the game. We can decide to take a lesson or buy some new equipment but that's all deliberative, rational stuff. But what we say in the midst of playing, that's the real deal.

But before going any further let's deal with the profanity issue right away. But really, what is there to say? Golf happens. I am not endorsing the use of swear words, merely acknowledging that many of us clearly find those perky little Anglo-Saxon words perfect for so many occasions out on the course. Obviously, in a strictly literal sense, they don't apply to what happens out there, or at least I hope not. If read as a transcript, a lot of what my buddies say out on the course sounds as if they were imploring their partners to have intercourse with them or that their putts were leaving streaks of excrement on the greens.

But used in their basic four-letter expletive form, they appear to help a lot of players when they need a succinct way to express their frustration. Extended into an adjective or gerundive, they add spice to any critical self-assessment. They're like salt and pepper on the dinner table: everybody's going to use them, just in different amounts.

This brings to mind a recent poll I heard about in which 36 percent of Americans evidently claimed to have never used the "f-word." Frankly I think there are only two possible conclusions to be drawn from such a startling statistic: (a) these people are liars or (b) they've never played golf.

Now, among the non-profane things you hear out there, the weirdest stuff is what we say to the ball as we watch it veer wildly off target. The first set of comments are among the most futile you will hear during a round, what I call Hopeless Flight Control. You're yelling as if you actually could command the flight of the ball, but as you yell, "Left!" the ball goes right and vice versa. Your influence over the ball's flight ended a second ago when the ball left the clubface, assuming of course that you hit it and not the ground first. But there you are yelling directional commands at an object that clearly can't hear you.

A variation of this is what I call the Greek Chorus and there are two versions of this. The first, and more prevalent, is the habit of members of your foursome to encourage your ball, while in flight, to do something that will improve the result of your swing. They'll all beseech the small white object to bend left as it approaches some hazard on the right. And then there are the guys I play with who can't be bothered with these sham displays of sportsmanship and will instead urge the ball to continue following its worst tendencies: "Yeah, that's it! Let's go in the woods!" or "Plug!"

Speaking of confusion, have you ever thought about what a non-golfer would think if they read a transcript of what we yell at our golf balls during a round? These people would have to be forgiven for assuming that they were reading the utterances of a movie director ("Cut!" "Fade!"), a gunslinger ("Draw!"), a driving instructor with a really bad student ("TURN!!" "STOP!!"), an artillery commander ("Hit a house!"), or even a desperate single ("Oh, be the one!").

A set of instructions that deserves its own separate discussion is what I call the canine commands, such as "Sit!" or "Stay!" These are said with more desperation than authority since, even as we yell them, we know that not only are our golf balls inanimate objects, they clearly have never attended obedience school. Our repertoire of commands even includes instructions for the ill-mannered or attack dog as well, since we've all implored our ball to "Bite" on occasion. But in the end the joke's on us, because once we've thinned a wedge over the green who is it who has to go fetch? Right. Good boy.

Another entry in the category of Things We Say To A Small White Sphere used to bother me in a way. This is the expression "One time!" that people like to say as a putt is rolling towards the cup. Being an overly sensitive guy, I used to take some offense at this one. What do you mean, "One time"? I may not be headed for the Senior Tour but I have made all sorts of putts before. If by "one time" you mean once this round, as in the Genie's only granting one wish, not three, don't I get to choose? But having given it some thought I've come to the conclusion that this is actually an expression of great philosophical insight. After all, as that snaking 18-footer rolls towards the cup, we are experiencing a completely unique moment in the history of the universe. Never before and never again will this group of golfers be gathered in this particular situation to witness this exact putt or shot. Of course somebody should cry out "One time!" because this will be the only time this ever happens. But then that raises the question why we don't yell it more often since every round, no matter how familiar the foursome, is a string of cosmically unique events: "One time!" as we launch our drive on number two into the trees on the right; "One time!" as we send our approach into thirteen into the right front bunker. And of course we know the answer to this. We don't yell it because it doesn't happen just one time, does it?

This leads to the question of how these verbal ejaculations (I couldn't resist using that word at least once in this chapter) have changed over time. Somehow I don't think that golfers in our fathers' generation yelled, "Be the club!" as a tee shot on a par three zeroed in on the hole. That just sounds to me like something that came out of the 60's-inspired notion about the game as an arena for developing a Zen-like focus. Similarly, telling your partner "You da man!" is not the kind of praise that was voiced as foursomes left the green in 1958, or '78 for that matter.

Yet another category are the stock phrases and clichéd aphorisms that are recited daily on courses around the world. One that always struck me as weird is the comment often made to a player after he or she hits a great shot: "That's the one that will bring you back". I never felt that way. The shots that brought me back were the ones I blew. I wanted a second (or a third or a fourth...) chance at those. Don't get me wrong. I liked the good shots, I just saw improvement as the elimination if not extinction of the awful ones.

Another classic is the sage pronouncement that "Golf is all _____", with tempo usually the leader in the clubhouse. Yes, tempo is important but the difficult truth about golf is that it isn't about just one thing. That's what makes it so captivating and maddening. Sprinting is all about running faster. Weight lifting is about lifting more weight. Golf is all about a whole lot of things, but that doesn't sound as wise as proclaiming the primacy of tempo or balance.

Another old chestnut that gets airtime every weekend across the country is the adage, "Drive for Show, Putt for Dough" which comes in two versions: the triumphant and slightly obnoxious pronouncement by the guy who hit a mediocre drive but sank a 20-footer to win the hole or the wistful commentary from the guy who smoked it down the middle but that staggered home with bogey or worse. Well, guess what? It turns out that even this isn't true. The professor at Columbia who analyzed over 43,000 golf shots from players ranging from tour pros to high handicap amateurs found that the biggest factor explaining the difference in scoring between really good players and the rest of us are the long shots. In other words if we were looking for the part of a PGA player's game that we would want to graft onto our version of the sport we would benefit the most by having the pro hit all the shots over 100 yards, not the ones inside 100.

And why would this be? Well, first, and as yet another example of how the rich get richer, the shorter hitter is not the straighter hitter. The guy who hits it longer tends to hit it straighter as well.

He's just better and so he gets to play a better set of second shots. Second, part of the basis for emphasizing the importance of the short game in scoring is the widely quoted statistic that 60 to 65 percent of all shots are struck within 100 yards of the hole. But the problem with this is that it includes all the "gimme" putts of two and a half feet or less. Take those out and the shots inside 100 yards drop to about half of your shots and if you eliminate the very makeable putts of three and a half feet or less the percentage drops into the range of 41 to 47 percent. The obvious implication is that if over half our meaningful shots are taking place at a good distance from the hole then that is where the dough is, or if you prefer, where the dough is being lost.

Finally, let's consider the fascinating topic of what we say not to the ball, but to ourselves. Now we all talk to ourselves to some degree, but golf seems unique in terms of being an activity where we decide to turn the volume up so others can hear. It's as if we've decided to let that critical inner voice get on the speakerphone. It's no longer all in your head, but instead passing through your lips.

Often what's expressed is a little outburst of self-criticism. We know our bad habits so well that we can identify their handiwork immediately. Of course this raises the question of why this identification couldn't have been preventative rather than diagnostic. But then, it's always been easier when playing golf to see things in the rear-view mirror than through the windshield. I've observed my own tendency to utter the instant diagnosis while the ball is still in flight, and in fact not even lost yet. I know this starts with a desire to be seen, if not as a good golfer, at least as a smart one. It's like an instant jolt of schizophrenia and I can't wait to have the Little Smartypants version of me raise his hand and blurt out the answer as a way of compensating in some small way for the Big Spastic version that just pulled it into the bunker.

With some of my playing partners these outbursts can be rather detailed. If one read a transcript of how some of my friends, at times, describe themselves during a round and accepted it as the literal truth, one would assume that I spend my weekend mornings with a bunch of morbidly obese cross-dressers who have the touch of a blacksmith and brains the size of a pea. (Actually, I exaggerated for the sake of a cheap laugh. Their brains are more the size of walnuts.)

But my favorite, and I think the most revealing, are the myriad ways that golfers, after an errant shot, address themselves by their first name. These little bursts of schizophrenia come in so many nuances of tone: anger, frustration, disappointment, and bewilderment. Trying to figure it out is kind of like wine tasting: "Did you catch that hint of scolding parent? And I thought I heard some angry nun in that last one."

And you can hear all of these and more from the same guy in the course of one round. It's like being on the set of "Sybil Goes Golfing." You're left wondering how many personalities there are inside that head. And if there really is more than one, at the end of the round you're really only interested in dealing with one of them: the guy with the wallet.

WHAT IF GOLF BALLS TALKED?

We spend a lot of time talking to our golf balls but have you ever thought about what it would be like if golf balls did the talking?

Because, let's face it, our relationship with our golf balls is fundamentally abusive. We smack them on their sides with implements made of forged steel and titanium, sending them skidding and careening off the entire spectrum of mineral and vegetable matter out on the course. They get yelled at when we do something wrong, but get no credit whatsoever when the shot is properly executed. Then it's "Be the club" or "I got all of that one."

But for all our apparent dominance we are the ones who have to follow them, and in the manner of the abused, they exact a small measure of passive aggressive revenge by forcing us to abide by the result of their final bounces and dribbles when they settle into their next temporary resting place. And like abused children, a lot of them just take off. An estimated 300 million golf balls are lost in the U.S. each year. Here's an example of what one ball might have to say:

"Hey, I heard that. What's with the aggrieved tone of voice, pal? 'Yeah I found it,' in that weary sort of way, like I'm some stray calf or runaway pet. You think it was my idea to wind up in this thick wet rough? Yeah, that's right. I just decided on my own while sitting on the tee waiting, cringing while you're doing whatever it is you do when you're getting ready to hit me, that I didn't want to sit out on the nicely trimmed fairway in the sun, no I wanted to wind up in some tall grass with my rear end sitting in some slimy goop. It was all my idea. Yeah, I'm real sorry. Must be my fault.

"Let me explain something to you. We come out of the factory and get packaged up like peas in a pod. And we sit there, waiting, wondering who it is who will pull our sleeve from the rack, open it up and set us free. Sure, we'd all like to wind up with one of the low digit guys, somebody who hits us less than 80 times a round and who makes sure we get a good buffing every time we make it to the green. But it could just as easily be some hack who's likely to send us crashing into tree trunks and scraping our skin off on the cart paths.

"But when duty calls, we are always there. When was the last time you heard a golf ball say, "Oh no, not him!" Never. Like good soldiers we answer the call to service.

"But, hey don't get me wrong. I may not care for your tone of voice but I am happy you found me. When we're sitting with our brothers in the sleeve we're always talking about The Numbers. No, not the ones stamped on us, Einstein. They're all the same. What would there be to discuss? No, we talk about the probabilities of the different fates that await a lost ball.

"Yeah, yeah I know after five minutes we're officially lost. But that's 'rules lost.' Oh and by the way, the five-minute limit? That's really touching. Says a lot about our relationship. Doesn't seem to matter that a ball rolls true for 25 feet on the last green to save par or flew with the accuracy of a sniper's bullet to get you a tap-in birdie on the hole before. Nah, five minutes and it's time to move on. You can go from caring so much about which direction a ball flies or how fast it rolls or where it lands and then it's like it never happened. You look for a while and then you reach in your bag and pull out another younger, prettier looking ball. Golfers. You're all alike.

"Oh so where was I? Oh yeah, I was talking about really being lost. And while I'm on the topic, let's get one thing straight: this isn't all about you. Oh, a penalty stroke. Oh now that's a tragedy. Boo-hoo. Try sitting in a clump of wet weeds overnight.

"We know that the odds of being found start to really decline within an hour of being declared lost. After that it starts to look likely that we'll be out all night with all these microscopic cooties licking and nibbling on our skin. The next day our best and often only hope is that one of those old coots who's a ball hawk finds us. Which is okay really. Some of those guys clean up their foundlings and donate them to the First Tee program. And after a career spent at private clubs and exclusive resorts it feels good to give something back to the community.

"But if one of these patron saints of the lost ball doesn't find us, the odds start to really decline. And then there's the tragedy of the rejected lost ball. The guys in the Titleist sleeves are kind of smug about this because they know there's a good chance that if somebody finds them they'll say, 'Hey this one's in good shape' and before you know it you're riding along in the warmth of their pocket. But if you came from the Top Flite or Pinnacle factory you have to prepare for the crushing disappointment of being picked up and then flung away as if you were a dried dog dropping.

"After a week or two even the sturdiest Pro V1 begins to buckle under the pressure. You know that eventually the mowers will find you. Oh the horror. We're told that it happens so quickly that you don't feel any pain. The worst is hearing the mobile guillotines approaching and having to wonder if this is going to be the day. But then again maybe the ones the mowers mutilate are the lucky ones. Decomposing can take hundreds of years.

"Oh and while we're on this gruesome topic, answer this question for me: what is it that you all find so amusing when you see a ball that's been cut in two? 'Hey, look at the slice somebody put on this one!' That's real clever. Hey funny man, here's a tip: keep the day job. And you wonder why we don't listen to you.

"And let's clear something else up. Yes, we enjoy soaring through the air for hundreds of yards, or hitting the green and spinning backwards or rolling across a green on a path that looks like a slalom course and then plummeting headfirst into a hole in the ground. But that doesn't mean we're adventurous. I have no interest in seeing unexplored sections of the course. I like the fairway. I like returning at the end of the round to the warm camaraderie of the bag room.

"But whoa, hold on a second. Yeah I know I've been going on for a while but what is that you just said to the other guy in the cart? You think you see a window? Get serious, man. Please I'm begging you. Just punch me out to the fairway. Take your medicine like a man and stop pretending that you're Seve Ballesteros. No, no, please don't. Oh my god is that your four iron? Where's your wedge?

"Come on listen to me. You don't have to resort to the miraculous. You're much better than that. Just punch me out to the fairway and then it's a simple iron onto the green. You can do it. I take back everything I said about this predicament being your fault. Really.

"Oh my God, what kind of practice swing is that? This can't be happening. What did you just say? 'Keep on eye on this one?' Maybe I'm not so glad you found me."

Swooosh.

Thwack.

Crack.

Plop.

"Oh and you're the one who thinks he has the right to swear right now? My forehead is killing me. That must have left a mark."

CHAPTER 7

GOLF AND TIME

One of the other hazards of the game is the question of time. Save yourself the expense of private club dues and you often find yourself mired in a six-hour round. Pay the entrance fee and the monthly dues to a club and you can still find yourself playing with people who are fuming because they had to wait on two shots.

One of the reasons cited for the decline in the number of rounds played (which is really just a measurable way of saying that the sport's popularity is declining) is the amount of time it takes to play the game. Parents these days not only have jobs that, thanks to the wonders of the wireless world, bleed over into the rest of their lives, they have obligations like soccer games or girl's sports teams that their parents never had to deal with or even dreamt of. And God forbid your child is actually talented at one of these sports because then you are sucked into the world of the elite team which involves weekend long excursions to obscure towns whose only attractions are a surfeit of athletic facilities.

I also suspect that golf's time consumption is another reason to dislike golfers and hate the sport. If you're harried and over-worked it's pretty easy to resent somebody who has the time, not to mention the money, for a game that takes four hours if things are moving at the recommended pace. This brings to mind one of the many paradoxes about our game. To non-members of private clubs, one of the first and most obvious advantages of membership is the ability to play as much as golf as you want when in actuality the real benefit is being able to play as little as you like on any given day. If you are lucky enough to be a member of a club there are few greater pleasures than dropping by to play six holes on a summer evening on your way home from work. My club, Lake Merced in Daly City California, has the traditional layout in which the ninth and eighteenth greens are right by the clubhouse. But a great feature of the course design is that the sixth and fourteenth greens are just a short wedge further away and so you can stroll out and play a quick six holes on the front that includes four challenging par-fours, the easiest par-three on the course and a short par five that offers, at least in theory, a good shot at birdie. Alternatively you could head off the back and play a quick handful of holes in a matter of minutes. Unfortunately this sort of option isn't available on public courses, which despite their equalitarian philosophy operate like stodgy prix-fixe restaurants: this is what we're serving, this is the portion you get and this is how much it costs. It would be cool if public courses installed some sort of scanning device that would allow you to drop in and pay a per-hole fee that meant you could play as little or as much as you like.

This brings us to the most obvious reason for the time consumption involved in a round of golf: the convention that a round is 18 holes. Although we certainly act at times as if it were the case, there is nothing divinely ordained about that being "The" proper number of holes. The number 18 was not on some second set of tablets that Moses didn't make a big deal about because he wanted people to concentrate on the first ten about worship and personal behavior. When Scotsmen first started playing the game courses were of widely varying hole numbers. North Berwick had seven holes. Musselburgh started with five holes and then expanded to eight. The First Open Championship was played at Prestwick in 1860 on a course that had 12 holes. Bruntsfield Links, the oldest course in the world where golf is still played, had six holes. As it happened a course in a college town on the eastern shores of Scotland had a layout in which golfers played out from the clubhouse to a series of nine greens and then back through the same greens to complete a round of 18 holes. The name of the course: St. Andrews. The emergence of St. Andrews as the pre-eminent place to play made 18 the standard for course design. Given that there was a course called Montrose that had 25 holes I suppose the golf widows of the world should be happy that St. Andrews received royal favor early on. But to go back to my point about Moses, this notion of 18 holes as the proper length of a course isn't derived from any sort of natural law or divine dictate.

PACE OF PLAY

But that's enough about that aspect of the relationship between golf and time. Let's talk about the one thing we all hate: slow play. And the crux of the pace of play controversy is this: having to wait on our shots. There's a reason coaches of the opposing team call a time out before a key free throw or field goal. If a professional doesn't like having to stew over doing something they've done hundreds of times before and have achieved an acknowledged level of mastery over, imagine what's it like for us to stand there contemplating a shot that the inflexible math of our index indicates we have less than a 50-50 chance of pulling off.

There's a rhythm to our game that we don't want disrupted: Hit it, find it, hit it, find it, hit it, find it, hit it, mark it, putt it, mark it, putt it, have it conceded. It's the soundtrack to the movie version of the bestseller, "Hit, Pray, Hunt". It's a real shame to break up something as finely syncopated as that. Golfus interruptus is just another form of fun control.

But isn't it interesting that waiting is such an issue in a sport that involves so much of it already. When you're out with your usual foursome roughly three quarters of the swings aren't yours, and even if you choose not to watch all of them, you still have to deal with their consequences. This just underscores the fluid nature of time when we're golfing. There's good waiting, such as watching your opponent line up a putt that you know he's going to miss, and there's bad waiting, like standing in the fairway watching somebody in the group in front of you plumb bob a three-footer.

There's a lot to recommend about our sport, but let's be honest: there's a lot of standing around involved. I've always known this but it really struck home one day when I thought about a golf course that I actually have never played. It's a flat layout called Diablo Creek, next to the junction of routes 4 and 242 in the little hamlet of Clyde in Contra Costa County, California. I drive by the course six to eight times a week on my way to look after my company's real estate holdings on the other side of the Willow Pass. It occurred to me one day that for all the times that I have driven by the course I had never, not once, seen somebody actually hit a shot. Now it is true that I am going by at 65 miles an hour so I can't text and watch the golf course at the same time but still I realized that I'd seen lots of what we do between shots: standing in the fairway, sitting in carts, pacing from yardage markers, hundreds of practice swings and the familiar tableau of three players standing to the side while a fourth lined up a putt. But not once, as I drove by had I ever seen somebody strike a golf ball. At first I thought, "Wow, what are the odds of that?" and then I realized that given the nature of our sport, they were actually pretty high.

In fact, if the legend is true and the game began as a diversion for Scottish shepherds, there isn't any point trying to deny that golf is a big time consumer. That's what it was meant to be from the very beginning. Shepherds were the mall cops of antiquity. Their job was to watch a space populated by creatures that were basically roaming around, doing a little grazing. The younger ones were checking each other out and playing around and the mothers made it a point to keep an eye on the youngest. If you've got nothing but time on your hands, what better way to stay amused and warm than to hit a rock around with a crooked stick. Who cares if it takes all day? It's not as if you have anything else to do.

There are things we can all do to speed up the pace of play: dispensing with protocol on the tee and just playing "ready golf", lining up your putt while others are putting, getting ready to hit as soon as possible. As players age they could put aside their egos and move up to a forward set of tees. Every weekend across the country courses are clogged up by golfers of only average ability whose odometers have clicked past fifty years and yet they set out each round from the blue tees. I have a piece of advice for these guys: the blue tees aren't like urinals, the default choice because they're convenient and the first things you come to. Keep going and shave a couple hundred yards and more than a few minutes off the round.

Another suggestion I'd make is the elimination of "indies" when you already have a good team match. We've all got playing partners who can't get enough action and so after the foursome has arranged sides for the two-man match, there's always somebody looking for individual bets with everyone else in the group, including his own partner.

What this means is that the putting dynamics slow down into a U.S. Senate version of the legislative process. Everyone has a vote on whether to concede a putt and by the final holes the whole thing looks like the final scene in a Quentin Tarantino movie where everybody's shooting at everybody else.

The Fourth Dimension

Time does some funny things out on the course. But then again why shouldn't it? The laws of physics and biochemistry seem to conspire against us, so why shouldn't the fourth dimension have a couple tricks up its sleeve?

For example, time seems to contract or expand over the course of a round. No, I'm not going to get into some mushy New Age blather about being one with the moment. But I am referring to those short intervals of time out there that expand ever so sweetly. I'm thinking of the snaking forty-footer that sweeps up to the left and then to the right and as you watch it roll back to the left again it occurs to you that the line you selected as the best possible guess is actually turning out to be the exact line and the stroke you put on the ball was just the right amount of force and for those sweet moments you watch it tracking, tracking, could it? Could it go in? Yes it did! Once again you've saved bogey.

Or maybe it's the view of an approach shot and somebody in the group says, "It's all over it," and you stand there watching it descend wondering only how close you'll be. That is the magic of good shots, the way you ride along with each of the moments that leads to the outcome and time seems to pause or expand as you watch.

And then there are the other shots.

With bad shots time seems to contract. Often the only suspense is whether it's going to cost you a ball. The wretched spectacle of stabbing a three-footer past the hole? That doesn't take long. Or you know right away when you've hit it fat. Your hands instantly convey the information that you have just propelled the ball forward by an event that is more seismic than athletic in nature. Hit it thin and your brain automatically cringes, knowing that if you haven't already looked up, when you do the first thing you'll see will be your playing partners looking off in some direction in back of the green.

This is the reverse mode of the sweet anticipation that follows a well-executed shot. Instead, time compresses as your brain registers instantly that there has been a malfunction. Weird, isn't it that somehow the instructions you send your body seem often to get lost in the mail, but you learn about your screw-ups by way of instant messaging.

Another of the mysteries of golf and its relationship to time is the ease with which we can lose our tempo out there. The golf course can do to tempo what clothes dryers do to socks: send something we need off into another dimension. Can somebody explain to me what is so compelling about rushing a shot? As noted above, the total elapsed time spent actually striking the ball is a small fraction of the four or so hours we spend out there. Put another way, if a round of golf were a sandwich it would be pretty thin on the meat. But there we are rushing through a swing as if we had a cab waiting at the clubhouse. We can't possibly believe that these hurried efforts are going to save us time. Everybody knows that rushed swings are the bunny rabbits of the game: once they get started, they just multiply like crazy.

But time isn't just something that gets used up on a round of golf or, to be more precise, gets divided up among a bunch of component activities like watching the little palsy attack that your partner calls a pre-shot routine. We think of it not only as a quantity, but also as something that has direction. In Western society we see time as linear: it moves forward from the past into the present and on into the future. Eastern societies took a different angle and saw time as cyclical: from the vantage point of our brief lifetimes it may look like it's moving in a particular direction but in reality it is moving in a huge cycle.

Well, yet another cool thing about our game is that a round of golf encapsulates both these versions of time. On the one hand there is the singularity of the round and each particular shot. They are only going to happen this one time. This is it. There is a beginning and an end and a Judgment Day that takes place when the bets are paid. But there is also a sameness, for better or for worse, as well: the same sequence of holes, often the same partners, the same shot shape, the same putting stroke, the same initial hope that today will be the day followed by the drive home and the hope that maybe the next round will be the day. It all happens just that once, and yet it all happens over and over again.

CHAPTER 8

RULES AND HANDICAPS

So here we are playing a game that lures us in and then proceeds to press all our buttons. It entices and then frustrates. On top of that it sucks up major portions of our precious hours of leisure. It bills itself as a relaxing frolic in the great outdoors but can often leave you more frazzled than when you started the round.

And how do we handle a situation as messy as this? We do what humans have always done when confronted with temptation and competition: we make rules.

Now I would never call myself a cheater but at the same time I wouldn't consider myself a rule hound either. I'm not the kind of golfer who carries the latest copy of the USGA rules in his bag and I'm not even close to being the guy who can quote sections from memory. I get the basics, but I'm not into minutiae.

I prefer, instead of a strict application of the rules, an admittedly fuzzy definition of what they are, based on my own interpretation of what constitutes the spirit of the game. I've let opponents drop a ball and hit without penalty and I've skirted the unplayable lie ruling when the situation had no bearing on a match. The game's hard enough and I'm not out to institute Sharia out there.

And while we're on the subject of rules I would like to suggest one change and that would be the rule regarding the dreaded double chip, the instance when while trying to execute a delicate shot around the green or out of a bunker you inadvertently hit the ball twice. The rule book states that not only do both acts of contact count, but you are assessed a one stroke penalty as well. I get the principle but let's be realistic here. Have you ever seen this work out for somebody? Have you sat around after a round and said, "Hey, Bert, your shot of the day had to be that double chip on number fifteen when you holed out." No, of course not. The second hit invariably throws the ball off course and there you are embarrassed, frustrated and saddled with a bucket of extra strokes. Not fair. Just count the times you hit it and leave it at that.

But as a student of the game I will read just about anything about golf and that includes the latest developments in the rules of the game. Please understand, I don't seek this stuff out. Like so much other information in this digital world it just shows up in my email inbox. In this case the sender was the good old USGA with their latest Rules updates.

A few years back the subject matter was the 2006 Rule of the Week Program and I loved it! In case you missed it, in 2006 there were no less than 111 changes to the Decisions on the Rules of Golf. The email goes on to say, "While this number sounds large, only a few of those changes will have a significant effect on the way golf is played." Okay, that's cool. But since I'm a shallow smartaleck I had to wonder, if they weren't going to have a significant effect on how we play the game, why bother? What could they possibly be? And who cares?

But the decisions that did have bearing on the game, those were real gems. First was a "Relaxed standard to clubs which are 'Damaged in the Normal Course of Play.'" Prior to 2006 only damage occurring during a practice swing, practice stroke or stroke could be considered to have occurred in the normal course of play. Now, according to the more "relaxed" standard, normal course of play includes removing or placing a club in a bag, using the club to search or retrieve a ball, leaning on the club while waiting to play, or accidentally dropping the club. It does not include "throwing a club in anger or otherwise," slamming a club into a bag or intentionally striking something.

Now a number of questions and comments leapt immediately to mind. First off the clause about "throwing a club in anger or otherwise" is a little disturbing. I'm trying to come up with what qualifies as "otherwise." I suppose people could be filling up the time between shots by doing a little hunting by using their clubs as makeshift boomerangs. I've heard that the pace of play is pretty slow on some courses. Are people using the time between shots to make side bets on who can throw their sand wedge closest to a particular spot? Or are people on other courses attacking each other with clubs?

Also, I'd read that overweight people are feeling a little discriminated against these days. So it was nice to see that the USGA is willing to cut people some slack when it comes to bodyweight. If you're capable of breaking your club by leaning on it, well the USGA thinks that's "normal." Stupid, yes, but still normal.

But I also felt the USGA had definitely opened the door to some testy adjudication when it said that it's alright if you break your club trying to find your ball, but not so if you intentionally strike something. Now we all know there are two ways of using a club to look for a ball. There's the gentle pulling aside of some low-hanging branches, and there's the sweaty impersonation of Indiana Jones hacking his way through the jungle. And which one do you think is more likely when somebody's already three down in a match? Like they used to say in those old football commercials, "You make the call."

The next one was another broken club ruling, this time dealing with an issue on which I'd been just dying for some clarification: "What is the ruling if a player begins his stipulated round with 14 clubs plus a club that had broken into pieces during a previous round?" The decision was that the player "incurs no penalty provided he does not use the broken club." I didn't know where to start with this one. I used to think that the USGA was a bunch of killjoys with their two-stroke penalties for this and one stroke penalty for that. But now I was starting to see them as a lot more benevolent. First they were saying it's okay if you lean on your club and bust it and now they were out to protect the cretins among us. And besides who would want to penalize somebody in that instance? I'd be more inclined to give the guy an incentive, as in "Here, I'll give you a stroke on this hole if you agree to use that driver. Hey, take two strokes!"

(Before continuing, yes I realized that there could be occasions when a damaged club could come in handy. For instance that five-iron with the broken shaft is perfect for hitting from a kneeling position when the ball is under a tree. But even in that situation who needs that club anyway? Why do you think the Good Lord gave us feet?)

But what I really wanted a ruling on is the following: what else is in this guy's bag? Assuming that he wasn't carrying 15 clubs when the mishap occurred, he clearly can't be bothered to clean it out. He's gone to the trouble of replacing the club but the pieces are still in there. I bet you there's some pretty nasty stuff in those side pockets.

The final entry in this delightful bit of spam stated "that the distance between any objects, including golf balls, is considered to be a matter of public information and therefore not advice." Now I just loved that. It was Talmudic in its dissection of the issue. Of course, it's public information; just look at the distance yourself. What really interested me here was what they call the 'back story'. How did this get to be something that the USGA had to consider? Do they have people who are paid to go through the rule book and imagine what kind of disputes could arise if four of the biggest jerks in the world ever played a two-ball match against each other? Or did this question work its way up through the courts, so to speak, having begun in some real argument over whether telling somebody that their ball was eight yards closer to the pin was disallowed under Rule 8? Because if that's how it came to pass, I needed some more information from the USGA: the names and addresses of those players so that I can be sure that I never ever play with them.

Note: After writing this I learned that all these rulings do start as real situations that are referred to the USGA for adjudication. I'm still waiting for the names of those players though. And while they're at it, I'd also like the names of the killjoys who have nothing better to do but call in rule violations that they detect while watching a tournament on home on their new high-def TV. Is that what assistant principals do when they retire? And just to be clear, I'm not sending them hate mail or anything like that. I just want to know what that sort of person looks like.

HANDICAPS

The rule book may be the Great Adjudicator but The Great Equalizer in the game of golf is, of course, the handicap system. As citizens of this country we identify ourselves by name and Social Security number. As golfers we have an additional badge of identity: our handicap. It's the scale for the pecking order; it's the definition of the quality of your game. Dogs sniff rear ends, golfers ask about handicaps. At the first tee when somebody asks, "What are you?" the correct answer is not your astrological sign. Your demeanor, your sense of humor, or lack of one, will reveal itself as the round progresses. For right now, you've said that you're a 12 and the outcome, and in large part your reputation, hinges on whether that shoe fits. In real life our reputations derive in large part from our ability to be as good as we claim to be. In golf, integrity means being as bad as you claim to be.

Now the pre-round ribbing about the validity of certain handicaps is as much a part of the first tee ritual as the creaky practice swing or the mulligan. We probably all know golfers whose indexes are strangely immutable. The rest of us get monthly updates from the NCGA, but it feels like these guys paid their dues and got a tattoo that says "14 Forever." No sub-80 rounds or streak of "good days out there" seems to change it. At times you feel like yelling, "Hey, it's an index not a blood type!"

Now this leads inevitably to the question of whether all scores are being posted, but I'm not going there. For right now I'm going to assume that everybody's doing the right thing. After all, there is the golf club version of the 'perp' walk: the escorted visit to the NCGA computer on the part of the 14 handicapper who just shot a 78.

But while we're on the topic of posting I do have one petty complaint. At the top of my list of 'Things Computers Do That Aren't That Impressive' is the announcement at the bottom of the NCGA screen that the score you just posted is "higher than normal." Really? I hadn't noticed. Now that you mention it, the difference between my score today and par is about twice my index. How about that! Gosh, that's amazing. Thank you, Mr. Computer, for doing that calculation and pointing that out.

Even though the handicap system levels the playing field, it still doesn't do much to reorganize our foursomes. Handicaps may make it possible for a 20 to tee it up with a 3, but it doesn't make it any more likely. Left to their own devices, golfers tend to gravitate to others of comparable ability. As a result, golfers of lesser skill are spared an even greater than normal dose of humiliation, and the better player doesn't have to witness a particularly egregious desecration of the game. I know there are exceptions to this, and one of happiest is the opportunity handicaps create for friendly intergenerational competition. One of the truly great things about our sport is the friendly parent-child match, which begins with parental munificence, and then in my case, all too quickly degenerated to paternal begging. But most of the time, the net effect of handicaps in our regular games is the exchange of at most a handful of strokes. You may love your golfing buddies but there are three words you never like hearing them say: "Five for four."

Now one of the more interesting statements golfers have been known to make is the expression of relief that some low scores are finally going to expire and no longer be used to calculate their index. This is yet another of the great ironies of the game. Think of how much we want to play well as we take that practice swing on the first tee, or the satisfaction felt after shooting one of your best rounds of the year. But there you are months later looking at those rounds not as a great benchmark or wonderful memory, but rather as a millstone around your neck. It sits there week after week on the computer exacting its unnatural gravitational attraction on your index, pulling it lower when more recent performances would suggest something higher, sometimes much higher. You see those scores with the unfamiliar first digits and those asterisks and marvel at them as if they were posted by somebody else. There's a sort of Rome after the decline and fall feel to it. You're like a barbarian clad in animal furs looking up at an aqueduct and wondering, "Boy, how did they do that?"

Past glories cast a long shadow in any athletic endeavor. But only in golf, thanks to the handicap system, do they have such a specific application. Consider, for example, the following hypothetical situation. I go down to Cabo and reel in a big marlin. It's my best day ever fishing, and I'll always have the memory of that great struggle and the feeling of triumph that comes from killing a really good looking fish. If I care to I can have the thing mounted on the wall of my home where it will stay until the day I die. The day after my funeral my heirs will throw it out, but I'll always have the memory.

But here's where golf is different. If I go fishing again two months later but fail to catch as big or as many fish as everybody else, I don't have to pay everybody else in the boat. But let me post a couple fluke sub-eighty rounds and I'm carrying that burden around for months. Interesting isn't it, that a sport that places such a premium on staying in the present allows the past to play such a large role in determining the outcome of our weekend matches. Mutual funds get to say that past performance is no indicator of future returns, and as golfers we may say the same thing. The difference is that we are held accountable to that standard, like it or not.

YOUR HANDICAP AS
OPPOSED TO MY HANDICAP

But this still leaves us with the question of what makes handicaps such an interesting topic? Why are they so controversial?

Part of the problem is that handicaps are a form of enforced giving when giving itself is pretty difficult. We're all familiar with the sweet little adage that "It's better to give than receive." What a crock that is. In fact I think you can make the case that when we tell our kids this, that is the precise moment when they first start questioning us. It's so patently illogical that the child has to be asking himself, "Wow. What's up with Dad? He can't possibly believe that's true." Anyway, it's a short list of things where giving trumps getting: summons, pink slips, and hickies. Giving strokes in a golf match is not one of them.

Basically, the handicap system is a redistribution program. Look at what happens when we have two players of different ability play a match. A bureaucracy decrees that in order to make things fair the person with more (i.e. skill at golf), has to give something to the person with less. Through the handicap system the governing authority for golf in your part of the world establishes the amount of benefit that the better player gives his opponent.

Like any redistribution plan, those on the receiving end think it's pretty nifty and essential to having fair competition. And those on the other side of the equation? Well, the best that can be hoped for from them is a grudging admission that it's fundamentally fair but that aid should only go to those who really need it and that the program needs to be administered properly. But what you'll usually hear is grousing about having to give something to somebody who didn't deserve it. Substitute some different nouns and a transcript of low-index golfers discussing a suspected sandbagger reads like a bunch of Republicans talking about welfare cheats.

If you think I'm overstating things when I compare golf handicaps to a welfare system, consider the following. The USGA adopted its first handicap system in 1911. The 16th Amendment to the US Constitution, granting Congress legal authority to tax personal income, was passed in 1913. So there you have it. The handicap system is just part of the scheme of changes that was introduced during the Reform Age. And just in case you think that my conflating the introduction of handicaps with the introduction of the income tax makes me some sort of right-wing conspiracy theorist, I want to make one thing very clear: I'm a left-wing conspiracy theorist.

One of the problems with handicaps is that we're being asked to trust people and that doesn't always come naturally for us. With your regular foursome you know what to expect. But meet some guy at a tournament or some interclub competition and you don't know if the guy's being legit. Sometimes you get an early warning. Let's say you're playing a match against a guy who says he's a twelve. When he takes his cap off you can see that the leathery tan stops right above his eyebrows so you're left to contemplate two possibilities: either the guy's a farmer or he plays a lot of golf. (The third possibility that he's a farmer who plays a lot of golf doesn't help your predicament.) You're left with the kind of sinking feeling in your stomach that you used to get at your kid's soccer games when everybody associated with the other team —players, coaches and families — were all speaking Spanish. Somehow you knew that things weren't going to go so well that day.

Situations such as this bring to mind the advice a friend once gave me that you should never play for money against a guy who uses the word "about" when divulging his index, as in "Oh, I'm about a 14." There's a maximum of three digits in an index and two at most for a handicap. It's not that hard to remember. Nobody ever says "Hey give me a call, my phone number's about 555-2344." The use of "about" implies an amount of wiggle room that could amount to several strokes and more than a few of your dollars.

Of course there is a way in which this lack of specificity about one's index is accurate. The governing authority within your golf jurisdiction may say that you are a particular "number" but there are certainly no guarantees that come with that. The computer in the pro shop may say that you're a 12 handicap, but you are really somebody who's capable, or if you prefer liable, to shoot anything from 78 to 94 on any given day. You just never know who is going to show up. As golfers we are more like a deck of cards than a fixed numeric identity.

GOLDFARB AND THE THREE HANDICAPS

So far we've discussed only the artificially high index, which is the camouflage used by that predator, the Great American Sandbagger, to lure prey into his trap. The other misleading form of handicap is the vanity index, the number that like a peacock's tail feathers looks great, but isn't of much use when it comes to flight. These indices are the result of a careful process of selection in which only the best scores are used. And therefore, they share a common characteristic with other products such as fine wine or perfume where the ingredients are hand-selected: they're all expensive.

This brings to mind that timeless golf fairy tale, Goldfarb and the Three Handicaps:

While on vacation in Hawaii Goldfarb plays golf with three strangers. Since nobody knows each other they decide to play a two-ball match in which they rotate partners every six holes. For the first match Goldfarb is paired with a dentist who claims that he's a 10, but he tops his drive twice and three-putts four times. "His handicap is way too low," Goldfarb mutters to himself. The dentist insists on pressing on the sixth hole but then double bogeys. Goldfarb is already down $20.

For the next six holes, Goldfarb is paired with a lawyer who says he's a 14. For a 14 he plays extremely well, and Goldfarb notices that the other two golfers seem to have forged a quick friendship, and he suspects that the basis of their alliance is the shared suspicion that they are playing against a sandbagger. "This guy's handicap is way too high," Goldfarb says to himself of his current partner. And, since Goldfarb is a sensitive guy prone to feeling guilty about even being suspected of taking advantage of somebody, he starts choking and he misses a four-foot putt on the twelvth hole to lose those six holes as well.

For the homestretch Goldfarb is paired with a banker who's playing to an eight handicap. The guy's definitely a good stick and Goldfarb says to himself, "Ah, now this guy's handicap is just right." But since they have to give strokes to the other guys and the purported 10 finally starts playing like somebody who could at least pretend to have that index, they lose the side and a press.

Back at the pro shop the players agree to meet up in the bar and settle their bets. But Goldfarb only has $20 in his wallet and so he sneaks off to the parking lot and drives away.

The End.

CHAPTER 9

DIFFERENT WAYS TO PLAY

So, like any game, we have rules in golf. And since the competition is indirect, and by that I mean that we usually don't engage in hitting, pushing or shoving each other or propelling a ball at each other, we have been able to develop a handicap system that allows for "fair" competition between players of different skill.

(This absence of direct competition makes golf, in a sense, an adult version of what parents encourage as proper social interaction between toddlers: parallel play. I play with my ball and you play with your ball. That way we don't have to share and there doesn't have to be any pushing and crying. When we're done playing we have something to eat and then when that's over we each go back to our own house and take a nap.)

But have we gone far enough? Maybe there are other ways in which we can tinker with the game.

A few years ago I was playing with a new member at my club by the name of Michael Kelly. As we walked up the ninth fairway Michael said that one of the things he liked about golf was that you got to hit the ball as often as you liked. Of course his observation was yet another of the wry, self-deprecating but ultimately slightly misleading comments that we struggling golfers like to make. It's intentionally humorous because he's saying that he likes doing the exact opposite of the game's objective, self-deprecating because he's admitted that this is what happens to him out on the course, but in the end not entirely truthful because like all the rest of us he does enjoy it when he uses fewer strokes. But his comment got me to thinking.

What if we didn't have this theoretically unlimited number of shots? What if the rules were that all players were given the same 72 opportunities to hit the ball and the measure of performance was how far you got on the course?

Obviously this would require a whole new handicap system. Your number would represent how far you got on the course when "playing to your index." Thus a 14.3 would be somebody who's picking up after his or her third shot on number fourteen. The guys that we now refer to as scratch would be 18's, as in "Oh he's a great player. Played for UCLA. He's an 18." In match play you'd still get extra strokes. On my home course an 18 would give a player with an index of 14.5 sixteen extra strokes, the par value of the four last holes. That way the less skilled player would have 88 shots before his round was over.

One unfortunate result of this system could be the potential for reinforcing the tendency of golfers to segregate according to handicap. You don't see a lot of 5's playing with 20's right now and it might get worse under this system. For example, if your round is over at number fifteen do you really want to stick around and watch somebody else finish? Generally I know of only two situations when people will watch somebody else play and that's when the player in question is either a professional or one of their children. And if you're one of the good players you might be even more interested in restricting access to your foursome. You might like the idea of keeping the hackers off the hallowed ground of your eighteenth fairway. It'd be a chance for you to get in touch with your inner ten-year-old, the one who said things like "Billy can't come in our tree fort because he's not part of our club."

Clearly there would be a lot of implications to altering the game in this way. At first I thought there was no question that this would improve the pace of play. How could it not when a lot of members aren't even playing the last couple holes? But then I realized that human nature is such that once you ration something people have a tendency to start hoarding, and that this change could have the perverse effect of making people agonize even more over shots because they realized that they were going to run out of them eventually.

Certainly marshalling would be a lot more straightforward. It would take on more of a Highway Patrol feel to it as the following hypothetical scenario illustrates. In this scene my good buddy Don Wood's cart has just been pulled over on the seventeenth fairway.

Marshall: Scorecard and NCGA card please. And stay in the cart. (Pause as he does some quick addition.) Well, Mr. Wood, according to this you should have picked up on the sixteenth fairway.

Wood: But, but officer please I was...

Marshall: Come on Mr. Wood you know the rules. Let's just pick up your ball and call it a day.

Wood: But Declan and Staley are giving me ten strokes.

Marshall: Oh they are? You really expect me to believe that? They may be Irish but they're not that stupid. Look, you can just come in peacefully or we can handle this some other way.

Course maintenance expenses would decline as there wouldn't be the same number of divots and ball marks on the finishing holes. In fact holes seventeen and eighteen on most courses could attain the pristine appearance of Augusta National since they would be spared the wounds inflicted by less skilled players. Over time the quality of play could improve as well. If you're a 13 or a 14 under this system, let's face it, you're not that good. With your rounds taking less time you have more time for what you should have been doing all along: practice. Look, you're not going to go home early are you?

But on the other hand, getting home earlier could help stem the recent decline in golf's popularity that a lot of people attribute to the length of time it takes to play. If you're not breaking 100, it's pretty obvious that under this system you're not getting very far into the back nine. So you're home earlier. The spouse isn't as pissed, the kids won't miss you as much. It helps get your foot in the door, as it were. Then, as you get better and get to stay out on the course longer it's not such a big deal because everybody on the home front is pretty much broken in at that point.

Also people might actually start enjoying their rounds more. On my home course some of the more challenging shots await you on the last handful of holes. If you're a 14.2 most days you're not going to have to worry about hitting from a downhill lie in one of the greenside bunkers on fifteen. You're already done. Ditto for the drive on sixteen or those pesky downhill lies on seventeen. Fuhgetaboutit. Let those arrogant 17's and 18's mess with that stuff.

The implications would go beyond our individual experiences. There's a very good chance that the overall image of golf would change to something more athletic or heroic. People wouldn't ask "What'd you shoot?" but instead "How far did you get?" It would make golf sound like mountain climbing. And if you got to say, "I finished," people would marvel at you as if you had reached the summit of Mt. Everest. They'd ask questions such as "Wow, what's it like to putt on the eighteenth?" and you could make up all sorts of weird stuff because you knew they were never going to experience it for themselves.

As a final benefit, TV coverage of professional golf tournaments would be a lot longer. Since the winner is the player who gets the furthest there would be extra holes to televise at any tournament where the leaders are shooting below par. At those tournaments they play on those easier desert courses the competition might carry over into Monday. At a tougher course you'd hear commentators saying things such as "Oh, Johnny this kid is just lights out today. I wouldn't be surprised to see him finishing on the third hole when this is all over."

So maybe we should think about this. You could make the argument that this approach is more appropriate to the world in which we live. Every golfer claims that he wants to conserve strokes, but we don't appear to be able to do it on our own. Perhaps the ultimate solution in a world of limited resources is to start rationing.

DIFFERENT STROKES FOR DIFFERENT FOLKS

Okay, I'll admit that playing to a limited number of strokes may be just too radical a departure for most of us. That doesn't mean we can't consider toying with other traditions of the game. For example, let's examine how we use strokes in our matches.

We all know the ritual. You compare numbers and then the person or team with the higher number gets some strokes on the hardest holes.

Yawn.

This is so linear and one-dimensional. Besides, in certain respects it's inappropriate, because it's so tidy and predictable when our golf games are anything but. On top of that, I have other issues with this mode of employing our hard-earned handicaps.

First there's something fundamentally dishonest in how we apply these strokes. Yes, your five counts as a four for the purposes of our match but that doesn't change what happened. There's a slightly sleazy revisionist undertone to the expression "five for four." It's like a Florida recount; you tampered with the results. You can call it what you like for the purposes of the match, but it was and will always be a five. You got on in three and two-putted. I saw it.

Also, isn't this post-performance adjustment sort of patronizing? It's as if somebody were saying to you, "Oh, let's see. That's a bogey and that's not what a good player would score. But for you that's pretty good, so we're going to give you a nice big gold star." Oh goody. Do I get juice and a cookie too? When does the short bus come and take me home?

So allow me to suggest a number of alternatives to this current system. Rather than use handicaps to adjust and thereby enhance the performance of the inferior player, let's use them to drag down the better players. Let's give them a taste of what it's like in our world. There are more of us anyway.

Are you really going to accept a victory on a hole because a computer somewhere decided that you were eligible for an adjustment on your score? All right, of course you are. But wouldn't it be better to win a match that was being scored even up? Well, I'd like to propose some ways of doing that.

First up is what I'll call the compulsory mulligan. Let's imagine that you're playing a match and you get one stroke. Rather than the tired old custom of declaring a tie on the hardest hole a victory for you, let's give you the right at any point in the match to tell your opponent that he's going to have to take a shot over. Imagine that he has just nailed his approach shot into number five. As he's cleaning his clubface and wondering whether, even with you as the Decider, the putt is going to be a gimme, you get his attention and gently inform him that he's going to have to hit that shot again. It was a great shot but you're taking your stroke, and that one didn't count. Let's see if he can do it again. Bet you he can't. Now that's what I call getting a shot.

The threat of your exercising this mandatory replay will hang over him the entire match until you've used up your strokes. And then whenever you do erase a particularly great effort from the historical record, it will irritate him so much that he's pretty much cooked for the next couple holes. That'll teach him to come out and work on his short game.

Another variation on this theme is what I call "Nice drive, I think I'll use it." This version is based on the observation that the better player is usually hitting a better drive off the tee. So let's say you're playing a match in which you're getting eight strokes. To your opponent this probably seems like some sort of Bolshevist expropriation but from your perspective it only begins to approximate the chasm that characterizes the difference between your games. So rather than do the usual, why not play a match in which you get to use his tee shot on eight holes?

Now obviously you couldn't have the arrangement in effect on a set of predetermined holes. It would be too easy for you to "accidentally" top it or send the ball careening into the first available tree. You would need something I call the "Scratch 'n' Switch" scorecard that would look like one of those lottery tickets that you scratch to see if you've won. So on the fifth hole, for example, both you and Mr. Big Shot would hit your tee shots. Then there would be a delicious moment of anticipation on one side and trepidation on the other as you scratched the box labeled #5 to see if indeed you were going to be hitting your second shot from a spot in the middle of the fairway 270 yards from the tee box while your opponent set out on a search and rescue mission in the trees on the left.

This use of handicap strokes would give you multiple opportunities to show your opponent that you really are a nice guy and a good sportsman. You could offer all sorts of advice and encouragement such as "Hey I usually just punch it out from there" or "There is a window between those two cypress trees. I don't pull always pull the shot off but I'm sure you can." If he starts to get discouraged you can be the sort of good natured person of generous spirit who tells an opponent things like " Wow that's a terrible lie right under the lip of that bunker but I'm sure a player of your ability can get up and down from there no problem."

Okay, so maybe these applications are a little on the cruel side. How about something a little more collaborative, one that I'll call

"Here use mine". In this system instead of making your opponent take the shot over, you make him use one of your clubs instead. Big putt on the line? Oh here, use my putter. I insist. Let's see if Mr. Hotshot can drain it using my obviously jinxed flatstick.

Now obviously this substitution of weaponry would have to be done on a "like for like" basis. You can't tell your opponent that he has to try a flop shot using your driver. I'm not some sadistic sicko. But, in that instance, he does have to use your wedge if that's one of the occasions when you decide that you want to use one of your strokes.

There is a certain logic to this approach. If your opponent really is better then a slight adjustment in equipment shouldn't matter. After all, it's a poor craftsman who blames his tools.

Now this concept of adjusting your opponent's equipment has a lot of potential variations. These can be of particular use in setting up matches between players with very different handicaps. I don't know what the exact number is, but for the sake of argument let's say that once the differential in indices gets above ten, it can be safely said that those two players are playing different games. But when the spread in ability and skill gets this large, it calls for more drastic measures.

One of the more frequently expressed opinions about the current state of our beloved game is that technological improvements in equipment are radically changing golf. Players are able to hit the ball ridiculously prodigious distances and as a result there are great courses that are no longer suitable for majors, and then there are the alterations required to make other legendary courses challenging enough. But aside from the USGA testing labs, it's like the weather: everybody talks about it but nobody does anything about it. Except to go out and buy the latest equipment.

That is until now.

Under my handicap system we start fighting back. If there's a match between two players whose indices differ by ten or more strokes, they're going to play straight up but only after the player with the higher index chooses between two forms of equipment adjustment.

The first I'll call the "You Won't Be Needing These" club subtraction method. For every two strokes of index differential you just take away a club from the better player. Remember this is only when there's a big difference in handicaps. So, when a two and twenty tee it up, it's mano-a-mano, straight up, just like the big boys. Except that one guy is only carrying five clubs.

The other allows both players a full compliment of clubs, but we do something about the golf balls instead. For every five strokes of differential the better player has to go back a decade in golf ball design. So in a hypothetical match between Ernie Els and a 36, the Big Easy would be flogging some rock they found in a corner of Byron Nelson's garage. I can see it now. "Hey, big fella, what happened? The swing's not looking so smooth right now."

And these two options are just a start. You could have the Garage Sale Bag, in which the better player gets a full bag and the latest golf balls, but all his clubs have to have been purchased at a garage sale. Let's get creative. We owe it to the game and ourselves because it's really not one of our finer moments when we say. "That's five for four."

TALKIN' ABOUT MY GENERATION

But changes in the game may not be matters of choice. We may need to change the game because of one simple fact: we're not getting any younger. This is particularly difficult news for us Boomers. But let's face it, when TV commercials start using songs like "Gimme Some Lovin'" to sell retirement planning, you have to accept that the game clock is well past half-time. We've all seen the articles about how the aging of this demographic bulge called the Baby Boom generation will affect entitlement programs and housing demand. Boring. Let's talk about something more important: as we age, how will my generation change the game of golf?

Of course the equipment will continue to evolve. We'll have shafts on our clubs with the flex of al dente spaghetti and club heads will be the size of shoeboxes. And the balls? Ah, well that's where it gets really interesting.

You see, through the use of nanotechnology they will develop the Holy Grail of golf, a golf ball that actually listens. These balls will have tiny voice activated gyroscopes inside them that will allow players to yell commands at their ball in mid-flight. But of course you won't see these at the more exclusive clubs. You thought cell-phones were a problem? All this yelling at balls to "Go left!" or "Sit!" would be so unseemly. That's the sort of thing that happens on those public layouts. Members of private clubs will, instead, continue to show respect for the traditions of the game and just swear at their golf balls.

But we're not going to stop there. We'll have our own scorecards. As the years accrue, shooting par for 18 holes becomes more and more like the Big Bang: something you never experienced that is receding further into the past every day. Meanwhile the indices and the scores continue to inch up. 90 becomes the new 80. But we don't have to take this sitting down, or even in our walkers for that matter.

Par is just a word, right. So we'll just have our own definitions. You youngsters can go on calling them par threes, but we'll know what they really are: reachable par fours. When I'm 85, and I rear back and crank a huge towering drive onto the green of a 125-yard par three I'll be putting for eagle baby. But why stop there? For a generation that prided itself on breaking the rules the introduction of the par-six or even par-seven will seem like such a minor adjustment. You won't hear us grumbling about those tough number one handicap holes anymore.

But the real advances will come with modifications to the golf course itself. This will cost money of course, but in the tradition of private clubs we'll make sure that the younger members wind up paying for it. The design concept will be something called Super Senior Setting or S3 for short. At each tee box will be a button that when pressed puts the hole in S3 mode. (Of course there will have to be some sort of security protocol because we can't have kids or other ruffians fooling around with this. PIN numbers or passwords are out because we can't possibly be expected to remember them. Instead, in order to activate the system you'll have to answer some sort of Sixties trivia question like "Who was the original keyboard player for the Grateful Dead?")

The main feature of a golf hole in S3 mode is that this whole bunker issue is resolved once and for all. If I'm still playing this game as my odometer approaches 90 I will have paid my dues and then some to this game. As a reward I don't think I should have to deal with sand at all. So a hole on Super Senior Setting will have neoprene bunker screens that roll down over every sand trap. That means that a shot that would have rolled into a trap just rolls off the screen and back onto the grass.

Where it gets more interesting is if one of us really crushes one and the ball caroms off the screen towards another hole. In a likely scenario I could scorch a three-wood from 120 out on the first hole only to have the ball ricochet off the bunker screen on the left and onto the second tee box where a group of smart aleck fifty-year-olds are teeing off. And how will I handle it when one of them complains? Oh, I'll just say something cordial like "Hey pal, you'd all still be listening to crap like Perry Como and Paul Anka if it wasn't for my generation so just stuff it. And, oh, could you toss that magenta ball over here, I'm out of this hole."

A final touch in the S3 mode is a pneumatic ejection device in the bottom of the cup. No more trying to get the ball out of the cup by using the putter as a pry bar. After a three-second delay the ball will be popped into the air. Since there won't be sandies anymore (see above) you'll get a spec if both you and your partner actually catch your balls as they come down.

And when we're done with a hole we just press another button and everything goes back to normal. That way all you young purists from Gen X or whatever else is further back up the generational pipeline can have the experience of hitting out of the front bunker on a tough par four to a front pin. As for me, I'll be headed over to the next tee having laughed so hard I peed in my Depends when my partner's ball catapulted off the front bunker screen and over the fence towards the interstate.

AT THE TURN

So here we are at the turn. Time to go to the snack bar, maybe get another sleeve of balls and hit the locker room for a little relief. It's time to take care of a little business before heading over to the tenth tee. So while we're taking a break I thought I'd provide two little diversionary chapters. We'll call the first one, the Men's Locker Room because it has more of a geeky, sci-fi feel to it, and the second will be the Women's Locker Room, where the angle, so to speak, is more romantic in nature.

MEN'S LOCKER ROOM

Have you ever wondered what golf would look like to an observer from another galaxy? Oh, okay, so you haven't. Well, let's imagine that you had. This is what a report back to headquarters would look like:

Intergalactic field observation notes, report XR45YG.

From: Zynode Beta59-4

To: Zargon, Imperial Overlord and Territorial Governor of Galactic Zone MW-304.

Your Excellency,

This is another in my series of reports on the diversions and recreational pursuits of the inhabitants of Solar Orbiting Object QX-3. Having reported previously on NASCAR racing, sumo wrestling and competitive eating, I submit this report on a curious sport called golf.

The object of the game is quite simple and just as meaningless as all the other diversions enjoyed by the dominant life forms on this planet. A participant strikes a small white ball with a funny shaped stick with the intent of knocking the ball into a very small hole. For a planet that has a distressing tendency to celebrate excess and to equate more with better, this game does have the redeeming quality of rewarding economy: the winner is whoever accomplishes the objective by striking the ball the fewest number of times.

But of course, the inhabitants of this planet are never ones to leave well enough alone. They will not rest until they have transformed the simple into the complex (refer to my earlier reports on religion, interpersonal relations, and the Electoral College). And so it is with golf. The hole is placed far from the starting point with numerous obstacles in the way. When feeling noble and good about themselves, in other words before they've started playing, the dominant life forms like to call this arrangement "challenging". But once they've started they are more likely to consider it "unfair" and "punitive".

The game is played in surroundings that are pretty, if one has a taste for this end of the light spectrum. In addition, participants have the option on most courses of driving themselves in little vehicles as they follow the erratic course of their golf balls. When played in this manner the game resembles nothing so much as what the dominant life forms call "doing errands": drive a vehicle, park it, get out, take care of business, get back in the vehicle and drive off to the next task. And, in yet another example of the fundamental self-deception that has contributed to the alarming increase in body mass particularly among inhabitants of the area referred to as North America, participants who use these vehicles call their golf a form of exercise when they would never presume to call doing errands a workout.

Most competitions involve a modest wager between the participants. The winnings consist of several pieces of the colored paper with which the resident dominant life forms are obsessed. Based on my observations the outcome of the match is usually the result of poor play on the part of the losers rather then a display of excellence by the victors. Yet I have rarely seen that fact diminish a victor's satisfaction with the result. It is fascinating to see the pleasure these life forms display when profiting from their friends' misfortunes and how even the wealthiest among them will become quite insistent about being paid even the most trivial wager. It makes me think that we need to reconsider what it will cost us to buy off these life forms when we make our move to take over this planet. Based on what I observed from watching golfers I think they can be bought off a lot more cheaply than we've assumed.

In theory, the participants play this game for enjoyment. Yet the participants' demeanor while playing is quite different than when engaged in other activities these life forms enjoy, such as ingesting nutrients and intoxicants, watching two dimensional objects on video screens (and apparently the bigger and flatter the screen the greater the pleasure), and of course, copulation. When golfing the resident life forms are rarely as happy as when eating and drinking, always more agitated than when watching their screens, and, most ironically, although evidently far less enjoyable, a round of golf takes far longer than the act of sexual congress.

Based on my fieldwork I would have to say that it is the emotional behavior of the competitors that I find most interesting. The dominant life forms pride themselves on their mastery of primitive concepts of probability and spend enormous amounts of their beloved colored paper on what they call "games of chance." Yet on the golf course they react to their shots as if they were in a place where the laws of probability had been suspended. Even a cursory review of most of their golf swings indicates that a less than optimal result will be the likely outcome the majority of the time. And yet every day I would observe countless little tantrums as they executed and then observed shots that fell far short of what they envisioned in the little fantasy prelude they call a "pre-shot routine."

It has become apparent to me that this game is another example of the difficulties the dominant life forms here have in mastering their tools. Despite their squishy and inefficient melon brains they have developed rudimentary technologies. The problem is that once developed, they don't know how to use them (refer to my earlier reports on television and atomic energy). I would argue that one should add the golf club to this list. They may employ what they quaintly refer to as "space age technology" in the manufacture of their golf clubs, but their pathetic brains cannot keep track of where that club head is when they are trying to hit their golf ball. It is almost touching to observe their child-like frustration at their inability to concentrate on this one simple task.

But in the end, the strangest thing about this activity is this: to play this game the participants usually return to a familiar place with the same set of partners and go through a repetitive pattern of motions. This activity is interspersed with frequent expressions of frustration and exasperation, and only rarely with outbursts of pure joy. In this regard this game bears an uncanny resemblance to what these life forms refer to as their "work life" and yet this is supposed to be a form of recreation.

I must confess that on more than one occasion I have found this behavior so upsetting that I have approached a player with the intent of telling him that his life is so brief and his hours for pleasure so few that he should try to enjoy the game for what it is and not for what he wishes it were. But the result is always the same. They shoo me away and say to their partners, as all these melon brains do when they see me, "Whoa, did you see the size of that dragonfly?"

WOMEN'S LOCKER ROOM

She lay in the grass awaiting his arrival. Her perfect white skin glowed in the warm spring sun. Delicate drops of dew nestled in her dimples and they caught the sunlight, sparkling like diamonds. A leaf fluttered down from the tree above and came to rest, ever so gently, across the logo tattooed on her skin, obscuring all but the first three letters of her brand name. "Surely he will find me," she whispered to herself. "He's pretty awful off the tee today but I'm not that far off the fairway. If only this leaf wasn't hiding me." But she consoled herself with the thought that as long as her T-I-T was exposed he would see her and know that she, indeed, was his.

After what seemed like an eternity she heard the sudden squeal of brakes as a golf cart lurched to a stop just yards from where she lay.

She heard his voice telling somebody, "I think I got it," and she shuddered in anticipation. She felt the leaf being gently removed from her and she felt a surge of pride that she was the ball of a man who would not use this private moment to adjust her position.

The moist grass that nestled around her made it difficult to hear all of the conversation that was taking place a few feet away. She knew that he was considering his options and then she heard his voice, strong and confident as ever, announcing that he saw a window around the trees and that given the lie he could get a good draw on the shot. In the possession of a lesser player she might have cringed at this possibility, but with him she tingled with the anticipation of putting on a display of the magic the two of them could create together.

She heard the swift decisive scything motion of his rhythmic powerful practice strokes. From the corner of her eye she saw pieces of grass flying in the air. Then, there was a pause as he took his position next to her. Aligning his feet carefully he addressed her.

The chiseled grooves in his clubface glinted in the sun. She felt a slight glow of heat as his club came to rest ever so gently and ever so close to her. But then the warmth vanished as his club pulled away and she knew that in a mere instant he would propel himself against her, launching her into the heavens.

It was all so sudden. She sensed the movement of his shaft through the air above her and then she felt his clubface suddenly upon her. At once she was airborne, spinning above and around the trees that had hidden the sun from her and now she was beyond them, glinting in the morning light, the arc of her flight gently bending to the left just as he had intended.

From far below and more than a hundred yards back she heard his voice urging her to "Draw" and she did, as if pulled by the invisible string of his will. It pleased her to know that she could give the impression of following his command; she knew it would give him special pleasure.

Then she began to lose altitude and as her speed decreased the whistling of the air rushing past her diminished and she could hear him crying out to her to "Sit!" She knew that he knew in his heart that would be difficult given her starting point in the rough but she forgave him, knowing that in the excitement of the moment he wished only to have her succeed in getting to the place they desired. With a thump she landed on the front of the green and then skipped twice before rolling to a stop on the back edge of the green, 25 feet from the cup.

Slowly the world stopped spinning around her. She caught her breath and waited.

She heard voices and then she felt the dull rim of the old peso he uses as a ball marker against her backside. She tingled with anticipation, knowing what was coming next. His strong but gentle fingers picked her up and then, wrapping her in a wet towel, he gently rubbed the bits of dirt and grass stains off her skin. Polished, she glowed like a pearl and he cradled her gently in his hand until it was their turn to perform.

He crouched down on the green and placed her gently against the worn edge of the peso. And then the coin was gone, and it was just the two of them, together on that smooth expanse of closely cropped grass. She sensed his gaze as he crouched behind her, following a line that led from her rounded backside to the destination that they both desired so much. She heard him rise up and felt the slight breeze of his firm but exquisitely controlled practice strokes.

She felt the slight shudder of the earth under her as he took his position next to her. She held her breath. "Any second now, any second now." she repeated to herself. Then, with a firm stroke the smooth face of his putter sent her tumbling head over heels towards the hole. The earth seemed to spin out from under her and she saw trees and sky and grass spinning one after the other before her eyes, and as if from miles away she heard him urging her on. She heard his partner exclaim "One time!" and she felt herself slowing down. The short clipped blades of grass began to tug at her skin. She felt her course listing slightly, bending ever so gently and she was slowing, slowing down and she heard him cry out "Come on, get there!" Then, just as she was about to wobble to a halt, the ground disappeared beneath her and she tumbled into the hole, releasing that sweetest sound in the universe.

"That was quite a birdie" she heard one of his opponents say begrudgingly. Looking up from the bottom of the cup she heard his footsteps approach and she caught a glimpse of his smile as he reached in to retrieve her. Holding her gently in his tanned strong fingers he held her up in the sun and kissed her.

All right so I hope that was refreshing. Are you ready for the back nine?

CHAPTER 10

GETTING BETTER

As golfers we are supposedly all interested in getting better. 20's want to be 15's, 15's want to be 10's and so on. Even if age has robbed you of much of your power and distance, you still feel that there are parts of your short game that could benefit from more attention and practice. And yet our behavior would suggest that we aren't always ready to do what it takes to improve.

Exhibit A would be the way in which many of us avoid getting any instruction. Never mind that the guys who are the best in the world at this game have a minivan full of people to help them: we're scared of getting lessons. Haven't we all experienced that sweet shudder of anticipation upon hearing at the first tee that one of your opponents just had a lesson? It's taken as a given that this person is already in trouble that day. In fact, most times this disclosure of the recent lesson is provided by the student himself as an excuse for his anticipated poor performance. This kind of experience becomes the rationale for avoiding lessons. The golf pro becomes somebody to avoid rather than to seek out. At some level it's as if we fear that a golf instructor will behave like an unscrupulous auto mechanic and that spending a little time trying to correct our slice will be like going in for a simple brake job and coming out with a new alternator, a new transmission and four new radial tires.

But of course, if we're going to be honest with ourselves, we avoid lessons for the simple reason that deep down we know we're doing things wrong and correcting all that is just going to take a lot of work. Better to trust to luck and a couple quick patches and some new equipment than to confront the brutal reality that your swing is all wrong.

Now some of you may avoid lessons because you actually like your swing. For many of you this affection for your swing can be explained quite simply: you never see it. I'll never forget the first time I saw a video of my swing. In terms of posture and stance I looked like some creature that was the result of grafting Quasimodo's torso onto the hindquarters of a dog. This thing looked like it wanted to move its bowels but was having a hard time doing so. And to take the metaphor further than good taste may allow, if you were my owner and had taken me out to the course, to, ah, do my business you'd be making a mental note to pick up a bag of the high fiber food next time. And the swing itself? It appeared to be the result of a botched lube job. Body parts that were supposed to be relatively stationary were bobbing up and down, and the parts you wanted to see moving had the fluidity of a rusty hinge.

Since you can't see your swing you're like the elderly shut-ins in the dilapidated house down the street. You don't do anything about the overgrown yard and peeling paint because you can't get outside and look at it. Others shy away from dealing with their swings because they sense the enormity of the task. They know it's not a cosmetic remodeling job. No, they're going to have to strip this thing down to the studs. And it's this group that has the best grasp of what's required to get better.

These golfers understand that the idea that we all have individual swings may be true, but only captures the end result and not the actual process of how we got there. We don't exactly forge our swings from raw materials. Instead it's as if we were all given the same swing when we were introduced to the game. The problem is that this swing was like something manufactured in a Soviet-era factory that only made one size and one color. What happened next was that we spent our formative years as golfers bashing, hammering and twisting this swing so that it fit our bodies and personalities. This is why a driving range looks less like a Concours de Elegance and more like an Eastern European Demolition Derby.

So, since we're reluctant to spend money only to be told that we essentially need to start over, we resort to other less painful ways of sharpening our game. One favorite is the tip at the driving range. Unfortunately, the driving range is no different than other places like a beauty salon or barbershop where people like to chat while trying to improve something. In all these places, advice is freely offered that is not always accurate or particularly helpful.

Advice out on the course itself is a more delicate matter. On more than one occasion I have received advice from a better player as we were about to tee off on the eighteenth hole. Since the guidance that was offered often made sense I was left afterwards with a curious feeling. On the one hand I was happy to get the advice but there was part of me that felt like a condemned man who has a great heart to heart conversation with a priest the night before his execution.

It was helpful but I couldn't help but think that things could have turned out better if I'd had the conversation a lot earlier.

Of course my advisors could have been cautious about offering any assistance because of the phenomenon of corrective advice leading to confusion and even greater frustration. Most likely they were worried about the remote possibility that things might actually click and I'd correct my problems thereby putting their winnings in jeopardy. The scarier scenario, and I've been there, is when everybody in your foursome starts giving you advice. Somehow a group consensus has emerged that this is one of those messed up situations that calls for a coordinated multi-lateral effort. It's as if you've become the Bosnia or Haiti of golf and everyone's decided that unless they act now there'll be a lot of needless suffering.

Of course we've yet to discuss the one true path to improvement which is practice. And to get back to where we started, practice is the only way that the lesson is going to help you. You've got to work at what you were taught. But the problem with practicing is that it's everything your regular weekend game isn't: solitary, repetitive and absent any opportunities to win a few bucks. Who needs that? And even then, many of us who do practice have a tendency to view it as a form of mandatory community service: if we just put in the hours the charges will get dropped from our records.

PRACTICE

But when it comes to practice there is universal agreement that if we want to shoot lower scores we need to practice our short games. And yet the vast majority of us don't. Why is that?

First off, most of us don't practice. That time on the range before our starting time is not practice. That's warming up. In fact it better not be practice because if you are using that time to "work on something" then you can be pretty sure that whatever that "something" is it's not going to come together out there when you're actually playing. Now if you head back to the range AFTER you've played that's practice. Or maybe penance.

In fact, speaking of post-round practice, there is some psychological evidence that this might be the most effective type. Researchers performed an experiment designed to create fear in participants: when subjects saw a colored square on a computer screen they got a slight electric shock on their wrist about a third of the time. Evidently this was frequent enough to create a somewhat lasting impression. (On a side note this does raise the question of just how the thin the line is between the kid who grows up to be a sadist and the one who does psych experiments: what is it with these guys and electrical shocks?)

In the next phase of the experiment the subjects were divided into groups and given "extinction training": they were shown the same colored square but this time there was no shock. The difference was the amount of time that had elapsed between being shown the 'scary' square and its accompanying shocks and the 'nice' square that appeared on the screen without any pain being inflicted. It was kind of a Goldilocks and the Three Bears type division: one group had the extinction training right away, the other had it after several hours and the third had to wait even longer. The best results were with the middle group which would be the group we would find ourselves in if we decided to go to the range right after the eighteenth hole and work on the wedge shot that cost us two strokes on the front side. There appears to be a window in which the brain can edit memories and it's not when they're right out of the oven and it's definitely not after they've hardened in place.

(At this point I have to make a disclosure: I have no idea if this actually works as far as golf is concerned. When I'm done playing I'm hungry, thirsty and usually owe somebody money. I don't have time for the range. All I've done in the preceding paragraphs is do what Americans do all the time these days: I read something on the internet and I'm just passing it along without bothering to verify it.)

Another possible explanation is golf's appeal to the little kid in us. We just never get over the thrill of making an object fly so far. Even a little wedge into a green propels our little golf ball so much further than the home runs and field goals that are the decisive events in the sports we love to watch on television. Who wants to hit boring little 15-yard pitches when you can belt it? Somewhat related to this innocent thrill is a more self-conscious and frankly vain consideration. Tee shots are, next to putting, the most visible displays of your prowess. The audience for your fairway and approach shots is going to be more disperse and your errant shots will produce even more private interludes in the trees and bushes where you find additional opportunities to perfect your punch and recovery shots. But at the tee everybody, all three of them, is watching from close range. And don't we all want so badly to look good at that point? We know the old adage about driving for show but putting for dough, but Lord knows deep down we really like the show.

But there are other factors at work here as well. The range is forgiving, but the short game practice areas are far less so. Practicing chip shots gives the immediate feedback that most of our attempts won't produce exclamations of "Great shot!" and a conceded putt out on the course. Similarly putts either go in, or in the majority of cases, don't. But the range offers this wide-open expanse that dilutes the assessment of each shot. What feels like a slightly pulled shot on the range is the approach shot that an hour later will put you in a short-sided greenside bunker and lead to a double on the fifth hole.

As we burrow deeper into our collective golfing mind, there is also the possibility that at some level we cling to a completely irrational belief that the short game is just a form of improvisation that is not the elegant form of the game. It's a "Break glass in case of emergency" type thing, not anything you want to have as a steady diet. In other words it could be that we believe that if we keep pounding balls at the range we will develop a "long" game that will get us on in regulation and that we won't need to rely on those testy little shots that those players of lesser ability, the mere grinders, have to resort to in order to keep up with us.

Finally, and most probably, we intend to practice our short game, we just never get around to it. Instead of practicing from the hole backward as most pros recommend, we approach practice like we do an actual golf hole. First there's the tee shot and so forth. The short stuff is all that activity that happens at the end and somehow we just never find the time for it. We want to make sure that we've got these full swings mastered before we take on those finesse shots, and since the mastery of the former never occurs, we never get around to the important business of getting better at making the ball do what we want when the hole is close by instead of 190 yards away.

GOLF MAGAZINES

Golf magazines are supposed to be one of the more readily available and cheaper means of improving one's game. But I decided a while ago that I was better off avoiding them altogether even on long airplane flights and in doctors' offices. One of the dangers they present to an impressionable sort such as myself is what I'll call The Unnecessary Tip. I'll just be leafing through an issue, skipping over the latest golf porn photo spread of some opulent new course in some far off corner of the world, and there it is, Camillo Villegas on How to Get Longer off the Tee or Dave Pelz on The Best Pitch Shot Technique. And that's how it starts. I get sucked into some stop action photo dissection of a technique that I really shouldn't be attempting.

In most of these articles there are several steps involved in whatever instruction is being offered, but of course I'll just skim it and retain just one or two of them. And then, in terms of actually practicing this dynamic new maneuver I usually have two choices. The first is to wait until I'm at the course and can try it out with a real club and ball. The problem with this is that by the time I actually get to the course my mind has condensed the lesson into just one of its components and it's a fair bet that I didn't even get that portion of it completely right. So I'll attempt the shot but of course I'll fail and then when I try to go back to my old way of doing it I'll discover that little piece of advice that I gleaned from the article is like a virus off some spam that's corrupted my golf game hard drive. Now I'm totally screwed because now I can't pull off the shot that I had before.

My other alternative is to try the move sans club and ball. But of course this approach provides zero feedback in terms of actual results. The only feedback I get is from my wife who's never been particularly fond of my habit of doing this sort of thing while we're in a shopping mall.

The following excerpt from the 50th anniversary edition of *Golf Magazine* best illustrates the other major problem with these magazines. It was in the section with the different colored paper that's devoted to tips for the senior golfer, the short hitter, the low handicapper and so on. This particular bit of instruction was titled "Clean up Your Cluttered Mind" and I will quote it in its entirety:

"Are you thinking too much while you're over the ball? Even if you have a well established pre-shot routine, it can be easy to let yourself slide into a distracting thought pattern as you prepare to execute your shot. Before you start your backswing, your mind should be calm and focused on the task at hand. You shouldn't be thinking about your next mortgage payment or what snack to order at the turn."

(The illustration showed a guy addressing the ball but between him and the hole were rectangular photos showing a burger and fries, a house with a big dollar sign in front of it, and the logo from the X-men movies. Wow, I'd never really considered the possibility that my playing partners were thinking about superheroes in tights.)

"The most successful players are those who can eliminate superfluous thoughts before approaching the ball. To ease yourself into this kind of state of focused concentration, make a habit of thinking about the different aspects of your shot before you address the ball. Estimate your distance, test the wind, analyze your lie, and take into account the pin position as you approach your ball from your previous shot, rather than starting the process when you get there."

(Oh, so now I get the X-men thing. This guy is thinking about the X-men because he would like to have superhuman powers as well. In this case he'd like to be able to analyze his lie and the wind and distance before he even gets to his ball!)

"This will allow you to calmly choose the appropriate club and strategy for the upcoming shot, and to confidently stand over the ball thinking only of the target. Make this a habit, and you'll be amazed at your new found precision and consistency."

If only I'd known that it could be so easy to just think about my next shot and just be confident about my swing! You know it's a real shame that such clear, concise advice is only dispensed to people seeking something as trivial as an improved golf game. Who knew it could be this simple? Insight this powerful needs to be unleashed on the other more serious problems confronting people in today's world: Are you drinking too much? Decide that you want to drink less and just cut down on the number of drinks you have. Is your marriage in trouble? Decide that you and your spouse are going to start getting along better. Unemployed? Decide that you're going to get a job and go out and find one. See, wasn't that easy?

GADGETS AND DEVICES

There are also the gadgets that are supposed to help us and the most prevalent these days is the distance finder. There is something endearing about watching a 16-handicapper tell his partner, a player of similar ability, that the pin is "156, no wait, hold on, it's, ah, 152." It's kind of like watching kids play cops and robbers. Let's get real here folks. Does either one of these guys really know what that difference of four yards means in terms of the swing they are about to apply to the ball? In their quasi-competent hands their golf clubs are hardly laser- calibrated devices that can identify a target and take it out from long distance. We're not talking shock and awe here folks. It's more like hack and gag.

I certainly can't speak for really accomplished golfers, but I do feel that for most of us the range of distance for each of our clubs is less like an address and more like an area code. The pitching wedge corresponds to my immediate vicinity, the seven-iron covers an area slightly farther away and the three-wood is definitely a long distance call. Because of this I think it would be appropriate to see some product differentiation in the range finder business. First, I think they should market cheaper ones for the average mid-teens handicapper that just give you the first two digits of the distance: now the 16-handicapper is advising his buddy that the pin is about 150 yards and that's really about all he needs to know. Also, a range finder that rounds up would help cure our tendency to under-club ourselves.

The other product I would like to see is a range finder that is a combination of distance finder and medical device. You'd hold it in your hand and while it was doing its GPS triangulation it would also be monitoring your heart rate and the moisture content in your fingertips. It would have a read out like that old toy from the sixties, the 8-ball. You'd flip it over, and based not only on the satellite input but also an assessment of your metabolic rate, it would give you the advice you really need at that moment, like "Not today" or "Don't count on it."

While we're on the topic of golf aids that haven't been developed there's yet another one I'd like to see. I read once that scientists have been developing a drug for trauma victims that erases painful or traumatic memories, a sort of amnesia elixir. We've all seen the public service announcements that the PGA tour puts out about charitable work and giving back to the community but I think this is an instance when we, the average Joes who are the fans, can step up and put ourselves in the service of science. I for one would be happy to participate in the tests to see if small amounts of this stuff could be used on the golf course. Imagine how great this could be. No longer would you stand over the bunker shot you just screwed up two holes ago saying to yourself "Here we go again." What do you mean "again"? Every four-footer to halve a hole would be just a four-foot putt, not a replay of the one you've missed twice already that day.

Of course there's the risk of overdose and I suppose they'd have to pin a note on my shirt with my name and locker number on it. There's also the consideration of how to administer the drug. Just a pinch between my cheek and gum? Do I drink it? Snort it? What if they soaked a special kind of tape in a liquid form of the drug and it could be absorbed through the skin? Think of wrapping the grip of your putter in that stuff. Or if they could soak cigars in it I might actually consider smoking them. But then again, when I really stop and think about it, the nature of my relationship with the game points to the perfect mode of application: an enema.

THE REALITY OF IMPROVEMENT

But perhaps our failure to do what it takes to get better indicates something other than mere sloth or ignorance. Maybe at some level we just don't want to get better. It could be that our minds perceive the cruel logic of improvement and opt instead for the familiar frustrations and pleasures of our usual game.

And what do I mean by the cruel logic of improvement? Allow me to illustrate.

As your club head approaches the ball a range of possible outcomes fans out in front of you. In the future that is a fraction of a second away you will, like it or not, have selected just one out of an almost infinite array of possible shots.

At one end of the spectrum is the complete whiff, the Absolute Zero of golf. Then moving from left to right (or if you're playing in Hebrew from right to left), you start progressing through the myriad ways in which you manage to propel the ball in some direction, beginning with the swing that still misses but manages to advance the ball only because it happened to be sitting on the chunk of turf you gouged out of the surface of the planet.

This is the end of the spectrum where you find all the shots that result from administering a glancing blow to the ball, as well as those that occur when you make contact with something other than the clubface. It is here among the run of the mill topped and skulled that you can find some truly remarkable specimens, those Crappy Golfer Stunt Shots that we have all executed or witnessed at some point. One of my personal favorites is the swing with a fairway wood that tops the ball imparting so much spin that the ball pops up in the air and can actually go backward in some instances.

But I digress. As you move through this spectrum you advance in microscopic increments from the atrocious to the athletic but still bad, then on to the adequate and finally to the golden end of the rainbow, the abode of the improbably perfect such as the 240 yard fairway wood that rolls in for double eagle.

It is worth noting that as you make your own personal journey along this learning curve your objective as a student of the game actually changes. In the beginning what you really want is inconsistency. You want the perfectly struck five-iron that appears out of nowhere. Consistency at your level would mean a seemingly endless array of poor shots. But as you get better the objective shifts and you, like the uncounted millions before you, start on the quest for the Holy Grail of Golf, consistency.

So, with this concept of the golf spectrum as our new yardstick, what does it mean to get better? I'll tell you what it means. Getting better means that you just get dissatisfied with a larger and larger percentage of shots on that spectrum. There's less and less that's going to make you happy. Now how's that for putting a positive spin on something?

But seriously, think about what it's like watching the pros. You watch some guy hitting his approach on some ridiculously tough par-four and when he gets to the green he looks like someone who just got a margin call because he has a 25-foot putt for birdie. These guys get on par fives in two so often that they hardly ever look excited about it. It could be 590 yards from tee to green but there's Johnny Miller making some positive affirmation such as "Oh, he's left himself quite a putt there."

I don't know about you but I absolutely hate it when I leave myself an eagle putt of longer than 15 feet. That's when I really start talking to myself. Why do I even bother coming out and playing if that's the kind of aggravation I'm going to put myself through?

Clearly being one of the great players of this game means not merely accepting this escalation of standards but embracing it. I remember hearing that Ben Hogan said that his marathon sessions at the range usually resulted in his hitting just one shot exactly the way he wanted. Actually, that is something that I can relate to, but only because I'm not that good. Think about being as great as Hogan and feeling that way about your time on the driving range.

If you prefer something more contemporary, consider the following quote from Tiger Woods when asked to discuss his best shots of 2006: "It was a practice session I had at the Western when I hit balls about three hours out there. I had about an hour where I really hit it. That was fun. I had every shape, shot, height, spin, whatever you wanted. I had it for about an hour. That's what you're always looking for."

One shot per session. One hour out of a year. Wow, I'm so glad I took up this game.

Of course very few of us have the three "T's" that it takes to pursue the perfect shot: talent, temperament and time. After considering how these two legends of the game feel about their practice sessions, it's worth noting that most of us have quite the opposite feeling about our time at the driving range. One of the most frequent laments one hears from golfers is consternation over why they hit it so much better on the range.

There are two ways to explain this. First is the possibility that you really weren't hitting it better, it just felt that way as you pounded balls into the forgiving expanse of the range. "Pretty close" to your target on the range could equate to a downhill lie in a greenside bunker out on the course. The other explanation is that we get lulled into complacency at the range. It's like taking a course pass/fail. It's a lot easier to put a relaxed swing on the ball when you have a mound of mulligans at your feet.

The flavor of our practice sessions is decidedly different from those of the game's legends because we don't bring the same demanding evaluation to the execution of each shot. But that's okay, because remember the premise we started with: we really don't want to get better.

No, our quest is slightly different. Some of us may still be pretty immature at times, but hopefully we've grown up since the days when we were shooting baskets with our friends and the shot we heaved up from the corner of the driveway was the buzzer beater to win the NBA championship. Our fantasies are a lot humbler, at least as far as sports are concerned. We know our limitations.

In the end we don't want to be better, just better versions of ourselves. Hitting great shots would be nice, but just hitting more shots that we consider good without having our standards creep upward would be just right. Let the chosen few pursue that elusive perfect swing. The rest of us will go out to play having learned to accept that to err is human and that to do it as a form of recreation is to golf.

THE STALEY SYSTEM

All this raises the possibility that what we could really understand and embrace fully is not more advice about how to get better but something more familiar: a clarification of how to play more poorly. Now I have to admit that normally I wouldn't be inclined to share my secrets with everybody, but since you've read this far I thought I'd share them with you. So here it is, from tee to green, The Staley System.

Tee shots: A higher index requires higher scores so you're going to have to focus on this from the first tee on. And erratic drives are the foundation for big numbers on your scorecard. Most importantly, it's simply not enough just to have a swing thought. You have to be trying to focus on something in your takeaway so that you can be distracted by self-evaluation during that other part of your swing that actually involves hitting the ball. Or to put it another way, just make sure that you're "working on something" with your swing whenever you're hitting any tee shot. Two of my favorites, and they've been working great as of late, are to ask myself "Hey, did I just reverse pivot?" and "Was that a good shoulder turn or it was all arms again?" Try these and I guarantee you'll soon be generating that internal mixture of distraction and self-doubt that getting to a higher index is going to require. Remember this: the key is to think of your golf swing not as an athletic act but a mechanical process. Don't think Fred Couples. Think the Tin Man in the Wizard of Oz.

Fairway woods and long irons: Now if you followed my advice off the tee you've set the stage nicely for this next set of shots. Most likely you're not in the fairway and, if by chance you are, there's probably a lot of real estate between you and the green. So the operative thought here, and this is where these clubs come in handy, is to think, "Wow, I've got to make up a lot of ground on this shot." That's it, now we're thinking like a high handicapper. And that, of course, means swinging as hard as possible.

Middle and short irons: This is getting exciting isn't it? We're getting closer to what some other instructors call the Scoring Zone, but my philosophy is that you can add strokes to your game anywhere, so let's not forget these clubs. What's critical here is to shift the way you think about distance out on the course. Yeah, you've swatted a couple shots and now you could knock it up on the green, but stop and think for a minute. 150 yards isn't that far in the game of golf, but if somebody hit a baseball that far it would be a tape measure home run. And did you ever think about how small the head of your seven-iron is? It's not that much bigger than the ball, so you're going to have to tighten your grip and swing really fast.

(I know that all this talk about swinging hard may seem repetitive and it may be tough for some of you to put into practice. But take it from me: just stick with it and pretty soon you'll start seeing results!)

Wedges and the short game: At last, the Promised Land! Despite following my advice you might actually be right off the green in the number of strokes that good players call "regulation." But it's never too late to add strokes to your score on any hole. You can add them really quickly around the green, so let's get to work. There are a lot of tricky little shots here and your first response in most situations is to think, "Man, I can't hit this shot!" And you want to know something? You're right: you can't.

Now keeping the sort of mental attitude that leads to higher scores isn't always easy and you may find yourself feeling comfortable with a particular chip shot or pitch. What I've found works in this situation is to tell myself "Well, this is an easy shot so I better not screw it up." If you keep thinking about golf shots just as golf shots you're never going to get your index up as high as possible. You've got to make each shot critical not only to your score but your self-esteem, otherwise you're not going to get the tension in your hands and upper body that a High Index Short Game requires. Here's a tip that might help: don't let the distance between your ball and the hole determine how hard you hit the ball when you're chipping or pitching. Let the situation dictate the level of tension in your grip and stance. Do you need to get up and down to halve the hole? Is this the 18th hole? If so, you're in luck! Just grip the club as tightly as you can and let the tension in your upper body do its magic. There you go!

Putting: The beauty of the Staley System to Higher Scores is that the most critical component to getting your scores up is actually the simplest to teach. When it comes to putting you only need one thought: good putting is impossible. You've watched enough golf to see the best players in the world miss short ones, and if they can't make them all, what chance do you have? That's right. None!

The putting performance that you're looking for is just a question of focus. Focus on the incredibly small margin of error involved in putting. Focus on the imperfections on the green or the difference in speed from the last time you played. Above all, focus on the significance of the putt for your score or the match.

I know that I've probably made this all seem incredibly simple and straightforward and you're probably saying to yourself, "Come on Paul it can't be that easy! You mean if I just follow these simple pieces of advice I can shoot much higher scores?" And you'd be both right and wrong. Believe me, just following these steps will help, but getting the golf performance you're looking for calls for special preparation and the right mental attitude. So, as a special bonus, I'll throw in these extra tips:

Practice: Just say no. The same goes for lessons. You can do this on your own. Now if you must practice, spend your time on the range and, this is critical, if you do find yourself on the practice putting green limit your practice to a couple indifferent strokes on your way to the first tee. You don't want to have a feel for the greens until the fifth or the sixth holes at the earliest. It's critical to establish an utter lack of confidence in your putting from the very beginning of the round.

Mental attitude: I can't stress the importance of this enough. If you hit a bad shot it is proof that you're an idiot and have no talent for the game. Above all, it's important to see any good results out there as completely random and improbable. Don't worry if you hit a good shot. The feeling of satisfaction will be fleeting. Trust me. One affirmation that I've found to be really effective after I've hit a particular shot well several times in a row is to take refuge in the concept of the reversion to the mean. If I tell myself that things have to catch up with me and that a string of good shots leads inevitably to some bad ones I know that I can bring that mixture of dread and anxiety that playing my worst golf is going to require of me.

And there you have it. Now go on out there and post some big numbers. I know you can do it.

CHAPTER 11

THE PRE-SHOT ROUTINE

But let's assume for the moment that we do want to get better. Even a casual student of the game has heard that a good pre-shot routine is a key to a better and faster game of golf. The actual sequence is left to personal preference, but the framework is usually the same: visualize the shot, commit to the shot, and trust your swing.

Good, I'm glad we have that out of the way. Now let's examine this pre-shot stuff step by step so we can understand why it doesn't work.

Visualizing the shot. There are two issues here. The first is what you actually visualize as you prepare for your shot, and the second is the effectiveness of all this visualizing as the round progresses. Let's consider these in order.

I know what I'm supposed to be doing as I stand behind my ball to the right of the seventh green. Yes, my ball is playing peek-a-boo in the wet thick rough, and it's a front pin with a bunker looming in front of me. I'm supposed to see myself taking a smooth assertive swing with my lob wedge, sending the ball aloft in a graceful arc that ends gently on the green as the ball comes to rest inches from the cup.

Wrong!

Now, if you've not had the generally amusing and usually financially rewarding experience of playing against Don "Big D" Wood and myself, you may not be familiar with the concept of the Chat Room. Big D coined the term to describe the wonderful mental process that starts when you're confronted with a difficult shot. As I stand behind my ball on the seventh hole the Chat Room is officially open and everybody starts logging on. First up is chilidip@aol.com, followed by dumpitinthebunker@yahoo.com. What follows is a great exchange between these two interspersed with some additional commentary from dontchoke@comcast.net and arentisupposedtobe-havingfun@earthlink.net.

It can get ugly out there. I know I'm not alone. I've seen guys' golf hard drives completely crash. Some Bulgarian spammer's logged on and it's an endless stream of pop-ups screaming "YOU CAN'T PUTT" over and over.

The second problem with the advice to visualize the shot is that after a while I'm just not paying attention. Now that's not hard to understand based on the preceding discussion of the Chat Room. If your pre-shot visualizations looked like the golf version of those old Drivers Ed movies about car accidents, would you keep on watching?

It's not that I can't visualize. As a male who went through adolescence long before the advent of the internet and cable television, believe me I've done my share of visualization. Oh, indeed. I have visualized many things, some of them over and over again.

And not one of them, not a single one, ever happened. Which of course is my way of pointing out that there is a difference between visualization and fantasy. One expresses intention, the other desire. In fact, the more desire creeps into the visualization the less likely the outcome will match what was imagined.

But there's actually a more fundamental issue at work here. The problem with the pre-shot routine is that after a while it has all the impact of a pre-flight safety instruction. Somebody at the front of the cabin is going through the motions but nobody's paying attention. And I think the reason for this is the basic unpredictability of golf. Bill Walsh made the 49ers' offense great by scripting out the first 20 plays of every game. I don't know about you but that doesn't seem to work for my golf game. Somehow, I'm not getting to the seventh tee at four under.

Somebody once said that 85% of life is Plan B. I think for golf it's 99%. And when things start going astray, we start resorting to other means of improving our game. We can turn to that endless reservoir of misleading guidance "Tips from our Friends." Or we can say things to ourselves such as "Hey, I think I'll get mad. That's bound to work one of these days." As the ship starts to take on water the natural response is to start throwing things overboard, and visualizing a shot you don't think you're going to hit is one of the first to go.

Now before we move on to the next phase of the routine I thought I should mention that there is a more psychologically oriented approach to our issues with the visualization process. It involves something called 'repositioning' that is kind of like deluding yourself only it's therapeutically endorsed.

The approach derives from Cognitive Behavioral Therapy and the relevant concept as far as golf is concerned is the 'hot thought'. This is the instinctive, reflexive notion that sets you up for getting tense and screwing up yet again. The cure is to consider information that contradicts the hot thought so that you can feel better and handle a difficult situation more easily. So let's apply this to golf:

Here's the situation: an approach shot over a hazard, a delicate pitch shot to a tight pin, a long bunker shot from a downhill lie (hey, let me know when I can stop...). Anyway, you get the idea.

My mood: anxious, tense. I mean what did you expect?

Automatic, or 'hot', thought: I'm going to screw it up.

Evidence that supports that thought: Um, years of experience.

Evidence that does not: There's not a lot to work with here but I can come up with a couple things. There was that shot I hit at the driving range a couple hours ago, or there was that time down at San Juan Oaks a couple years ago when I pulled off this shot.

Alternative or balanced thought: I am not a spazz. I've done this before, just not as often as I might like.

Now, just do it.

Next: Committing to the shot. Why we can't.

COMMITTING TO THE SHOT

So, where were we? Ah, yes, we've completed Step 1 of our pre-shot routine. According to the theory, we've just visualized a low wind-cheating draw, checking up right next to the pin on number five. But in reality, what we just saw in our mind's eye was like a trailer for a Stephen King golf movie in which horrible supernatural things keep happening to a Titleist.

But it's time to get moving. You've got a foursome in back of you that's going to spend the remainder of the afternoon watching other people play cards, so God knows you can't keep them out on the course any longer than necessary. No, it's time to do what you paid all that money on dues, equipment and lessons for: hit a golf ball. It's time to execute step two of the pre-shot routine, committing to the shot.

But why is it so hard, as the saying goes, to pull the trigger? One reason is that it's kind of like playing Let's Make A Deal... except that you already know what's behind curtains 1, 2 and 3, and it's all bad. Monte's waiting for you to make your decision, but why rush when you know you're not going to like the result? Look, prisoners don't sprint to their executions. There's a reason the movie was called *Dead Man Walking.*

Personally, I'll admit to being a procrastinator. When faced with a difficult or unpleasant task there's nothing better than putting it off. And that's not always a bad thing. One of the many things I do better than playing golf is taking tests. (Actually there aren't that many things; it just makes me feel better to say that.) I always felt comfortable with the advice that you should just skip the tough questions and come back to them later. I'm convinced my handicap would be a lot lower if I could apply the same principle to golf. Can you imagine how great it would be if you could say, "This downhill lie on seventeen always gives me trouble. Can I just play out eighteen and come back to it later?" And the advice from our New Age golf gurus that I need to "fall in love with each shot" doesn't really help. That's not the problem. My challenge is breaking up with the previous shot.

But I also suspect that there's a more fundamental problem here. At work I can be on a conference call and at the same time check my email, sign checks, and with judicious use of the mute button, have a conversation with somebody in my office. With so much of my professional life dependent on my ability to convince people that I can be in four places at once, should it come as any surprise that I have difficulty on a Saturday morning concentrating on doing one simple thing over and over again?

The human mind is an amazing thing. But I'm not talking about the genius of a Mozart or Shakespeare. I'm marveling at the ability of a golfer's mind to wander completely off the reservation during that brief interval when we're actually swinging the club. Somewhere between the takeaway and impact my mind has registered such relevant thoughts as "Did I set the alarm when I left the house?" and "Did the Giants really have to trade Joe Nathan?"

Has channel surfing affected our minds or is the remote control the perfect technical expression of how the mind works? It's as if my mind decides as the club head moves away from the ball "OK, that's all set. Let's go check on something else now. I'll be right back." And sometimes it makes it back in time, and other times... well, you know how it goes.

Next: Trusting your swing: why start now?

TRUSTING YOUR SWING

The third part of the classic preshot routine isn't so much a step as a state of mind. According to the theory I'm supposed to feel good about the shot as I address the ball. It's time for a moment of self-affirmation as I tell myself that I'm going to be okay and that everything's going to be all right. I can throw myself out of the plane and the parachute really ought to open. That's right, it's time to trust my swing.

I remember reading that when Vijay Singh won the Masters in 2000 his source of special inspiration was a note he found in his bag from his son which said simply, "Trust your swing." How sweet. Somehow that kind of thing doesn't happen for me. The only notes I find in my bag are last weekend's pin placements or reminders that I still owe somebody money from last weekend's game or a list of things I'm supposed to pick up at Safeway on my way home.

But more to the point let's take a look at what I'm asking myself to trust. Hey, if I spent eight hours a day hitting balls I might feel like I had something to hang my hat on out there. I'd definitely be spending a lot more money on golf gloves. For Vijay the difference between good and bad from 160 yards out is measured in terms of the length of his birdie (or eagle) putt. For me it's the difference between getting to use my putter at all and organizing my foursome into a search and rescue party ("I'm pretty sure I saw it come down under that limb").

The pros, through innate ability and hard work, have grooved their swings into things of dependable consistency. The rest of us? Well, it brings to mind that old golf haiku:

Look at my golf swings.

Each one is like a snowflake,

Bad in its own way.

The difference between a pro's swing and what I'm using is like the difference between barbecuing with a top of the line propane grill and starting a fire with steel, a flint and some tinder. One you can turn on with the flick of a switch. The other eventually gets the job done but involves a lot of grunting, sweating and swearing.

Which leads us to that age-old question, "Where do bad golf swings come from?" One of the cliché experiences in golf is hitting some hideously errant drive, reloading, grooving it right down the middle, and then having somebody in the group say, "Same guy." So how do we explain this phenomenon? I think the answer lies in what I will call your golf DNA. If you learned the game at an early age or just have the pure athletic ability, you have strong golf DNA. One good swing begets another like a series of photocopies. If, like most of us, you have weak golf DNA then your swings mutate wildly. The ball goes left, the ball goes right. You hit it fat, you hit it thin. The good swings don't replicate themselves, but quite to the contrary, start spawning these deformed versions. And what, you might ask, causes these mutations? Stress, self-doubt and an inability to concentrate. You know, the usual state of affairs in my head.

Now some of you may be saying to yourselves, "This Staley guy's amusing every now and then, but man is he hard on himself." Hey, I'm a realist. If I think the glass is half empty it's because I know I drank the other half. The golf course is not a place for flights of fancy and making believe that you're somebody you're not. That's what they invented the Internet for.

THE PRACTICE SWING

Of course the other part to most of our pre-shot routines is the practice swing. Now there are two kinds of swing out there on the golf course and I'm not talking about good ones and bad ones. I'm referring to this rehearsal and the real thing. So let's consider the practice swing and its role in our games.

A couple years ago my wife and I were down in Cabo at the Hacienda del Mar. It's a wonderful place. Our room, advertised as an Ocean View, did provide a vista of one corner of the Sea of Cortez. A more accurate description of the scenery from our deck would have been Bad Resort Golf View. I'm assuming that it's understood that the word "bad" here refers not to the course itself, which is pretty spectacular, but to the performance of the golfers I watched. Our deck looked out over the eighth hole of the Desert Course, which gave me a perfect vantage point to observe, among other things, the relationship between the practice swing and the real thing.

Based on a large number of observations I've decided that the current debate over intelligent design and evolution provides a good framework for thinking about this relationship. And just as in the real debate, I'm coming down squarely on the side of evolution. There was scant evidence of intelligent design at work here. All too often the real effort did not represent any sort of improvement over the practice swing. In fact, I'd have to say that I saw a lot of random mutations. More times than not, the fluid, relaxed rehearsal morphed into something far less attractive. That's not to say that there wasn't a distinct family resemblance between practice and real swings. The problem was that the real effort was more like a third cousin from Bakersfield with a drug problem: a couple more twitches, jerkier and definitely unbalanced.

Obviously these gringos tightened up when they were executing The Swing with Consequences. So what's going on here? I think the key to understanding the relationship between the pre-shot routine and the swings that count lies in the word "routine." Now you could say that the practice swing exists in the realm of fantasy and the one that counts is a return to reality. But the thing about fantasy is that you're totally in charge. You're like the movie producer and director: you get to choose and cast everything. So, in your fantasy, is that the swing you're going to be using? I don't think so.

It's more accurate to say that the practice swing exists in a state of numbness. It's just a ritual, something you've always done. After all these years it has the novelty of brushing your teeth, and you do it for a lot of the same reasons: way back when somebody told you to, you've always done it, and it's supposed to be preventive. But, as a result, it's the 24th slide in 90-minute-long Power Point presentation, or the list of associate producers in the credits for a movie. It's happening, you're there, but you're really not paying attention.

A lot of practice swings have the appearance of genuflections. Done quickly and as a matter of habit, they say to the world that you're sincere about what you're about to do but wouldn't mind getting a little assistance from a higher power in terms of pulling it off. This raises a question: do the baseball players who cross themselves before batting do the same thing on the tee? And here's the more important question: does it work?

So, having gone through the ritual of swinging the club while thinking about the putt you just missed or whether you over-tipped the waiter last night at dinner, you're confronted with the reality that you have to make a swing that's going to have an effect on the number on the scorecard. You tell yourself something along the lines of "Oh, okay, this one counts so let's buckle down and try harder." And we know how well that works.

So, what are we to do? How do we bridge the gap between the rehearsal and the real deal? One approach could be to bring the same casual nonchalance that you employ in your practice swing to the real effort. But a lot of us, myself obviously included, are constitutionally incapable of this. Not that I haven't tinkered with this approach.

Another possibility is to just make more practice swings. The underlying assumption here appears to be that if you have more good rehearsals then your real swing is less like a coin flip and more an event in which the odds are stacked in your favor. But there are problems with this, not the least of which is the pace of play issue. Essentially, if you do this you're just employing the same approach that salmon use when they're spawning: "I'll just spray a lot of these all over the place and some of them are bound to work." It gets messy and can leave you pretty tired and depleted by the end of a round.

Actually, if you think about it, the only way to bridge this gap is to bring the two swings closer to each other. And which one do you think you're going to be able to move? Certainly not the Real One. That's got way too much mental baggage.

No, you have to move the practice swing towards the real effort. In a departure from almost everything else in this book I'll actually pass along a piece of advice that I've gained from two great masters of the game, Harvey Penick and Dan McBride (the teaching pro at my club, Lake Merced). In your practice swing they both say that you should aim at a piece of dirt or blade of grass so that you're practicing a swing in which you're conscious of squaring the clubface at impact. Now you have a practice swing that's not as casual as before but is closer to what you're about to attempt.

But before concluding, I have to also pass along an obvious footnote that these two never mention: this doesn't always work.

CHAPTER 12

SWING
THOUGHTS

Ah, swing thoughts, the Post-It notes of golf. They're the little keys, the friendly reminders that are supposed to keep your game on track. They're the descendents of those words of encouragement and caution that your mother said as you went off to school: "Have a nice day and remember to look both ways before you cross the street."

Now, I have an admission to make. I actually bought a book of swing thoughts. How pathetic is that? I've thought about this and I can't decide which is worse, buying a book of pickup lines or a book of swing thoughts. The first is pretty cheesy, but at least the buyer is looking for suggestions about what to say to another person. With my purchase I was reading what other golfers say to themselves so that I could get ideas about what to say to myself.

Just to set the record straight I didn't actually believe that knowing what Fred Couples says to himself would lead to my getting his swing and tempo. But I was curious and desperate. And, in case you're wondering, Fred evidently tells himself to remember the smoothest swing he ever made with that club. That must be nice. The interesting thing about that is that Freddy has to choose between lots of very smooth swings, but still he recalls that special one and then repeats the experience. I, on the other hand, with a much smaller inventory to sort through, find it about as easy to recollect a smooth swing as it is to find a lost sock.

Swing thoughts come in several varieties. You're supposed to keep them simple; you don't need (and your playing partners definitely don't want you to have) something that reads like a NASA pre-launch checklist. There are the conventional wisdom versions: swing easy, follow through. The problem with these is that the teenager you once were years ago is now your inner golfer. And your inner golfer is just not listening. He's heard it all too many times.

Once it was "Clean your room" or "Take out the garbage." Now it's "Smooth swing" or "Keep your head down." Yeah, sure whatever. Yeah, yeah I'll do it. (Just not now. Definitely not now.)

The notion of your inner golfer as a teenager also explains why negative swing thoughts don't work either. We've all read or been told that you're not supposed to say to yourself "Don't go left" because your subconscious mind doesn't recognize negatives and will just hear "Left" and follow accordingly. Well, I don't know about you but my subconscious can definitely hear negatives. I think what happens is the old teenage self that is now my inner golfer likes to break the rules, go where he's not supposed to and generally make a mess of things.

Another major category is what I call checkpoint swing thoughts. With one of these you've admitted to yourself that there's a part of your swing that's, let's just say, problematic. It's like mapping out your itinerary and then circling the place where you heard that the road is washed out. These swing thoughts are very insidious because you're basically admitting that there's something scary out there.

I think anytime you start breaking the swing down into components you're putting yourself at risk. At times I've found myself thinking about my swing as if it were some trip to Europe. First stop, takeaway and back leg; second stop, downswing and shoulder position and so on. The problem with this approach is that I tend to lose my baggage on one of the first legs of the journey ("Oh, did I just reverse pivot?"), and then I'm just shot for the rest of the trip.

Another problem that I've had with what I'm calling a component swing thought is that once I've passed whatever checkpoint I've decided is critical my brain either goes on autopilot –"Alrighty then. Nice takeaway so I guess I'm on break" –or it starts evaluating how I did at that point – "Oooh look out, that was kind of unbalanced." Meanwhile the swing is still happening and the choreography is all screwed up.

It would be great if preparing for your swing were like ordering dinner in a restaurant. It would go something like this:

"And for you, sir?"

"I'll start with the slow takeaway and then I'll have the balanced weight transfer, and for the main course, ah, I'll have the solid impact."

"And how would you like that cooked?"

"Oh, on the screws."

Unfortunately, it's just not that simple. The mystery that is the good golf swing cannot be summoned with some little prayer. And, often the words themselves can get in the way. And besides, what exactly are we doing when we think about something? Are we thinking about It in all its "It-ness" or are we thinking about the not-It, all the things that we don't want to do? Or are we really thinking about the consequences and anticipating those rather than being present with the It that is happening right now? Not so simple is It?

Another problem with the swing thoughts that many of us employ, and this should come as absolutely no surprise, is that they are essentially too self-centered to work. Thinking about your hip turn or your shoulders or your right heel may originate in an under-standing of the particular issues you may have with the mechanics of a sound golf swing, but I've got news for you: it's not all about you. The one thing that matters is knowing where the club head is. You're a very important person in this process and you are in charge, more or less, but hopefully the club is the only thing that is going to touch or propel the ball and that is where your focus should be.

It is yet another paradox of the game that there is so much to think about in a golf swing, and if you let yourself you can get lost in thinking about it as you start doing it, and yet it is at the same time an athletic act and therefore not something that lends itself to thinking. So I've come to regard swing thoughts as the airport security of golf: they don't always work and they just interrupt the flow.

Playing like Bobby Jones

Yet, even given this knowledge that swing thoughts don't work that well, I still poke around looking for the magic incantation. For example, a couple years ago I was looking online for advice on the mental side of the game. Not for myself, mind you. I mean, come on, my game is rock solid. This was, ah, for a friend, you know, who doesn't like to use the internet, yeah, that's it, he doesn't like to go online so, ah, I was looking for him. Yeah, that's right.

Anyway, I found a place up in Marin County that specializes in this sort of thing. On their homepage they present their general philosophy about clearing your mind of negative thoughts and this included a quote from Bobby Jones:

"If I have two swing thoughts, I have no chance at all. If I have one, maybe I'll have a good shot. But if I have none, then I can play like Bobby Jones."

Well that's cool, I thought to myself, I mean I said to my friend. But then I realized that this quote was meant to be an affirmation and in order to apply it to your own situation you have to insert yourself, as it were, in the place of Bobby Jones. So I repeated it:

"If I have two swing thoughts, I have no chance at all. If I have one, maybe I'll have a good shot. But if I have none, then I can play like Paul Staley."

It was sounding so good up until that last part.

Playing like Paul Staley. That's pretty compelling stuff. Wow, imagine that! Just by following a few simple steps you too can play golf like Paul Staley. When you put it that way, I mean who could resist?

And of course that's precisely the problem. I don't want to play golf like myself. I want to play like somebody better. And I'm pretty sure I'm not alone in this respect.

But there appears to be a consensus out there among the golf cognoscenti, the gurus of the game, that the key to better play is to banish conscious thought. Read any golf publication and you're bound to come across items such as this tidbit in the NCGA magazine from one Dr. Glen Albaugh, former golf coach at University of the Pacific: "Playing the game without any conscious thought is important...you've got to learn to use what you have and trust your game."

For the sake of argument let's accept that this is true. Trust me, I wouldn't know, but let's just say that these guys are right. There are several problems with this.

First off, conscious thought is how I earn the money that pays for my golf habit. And I think I'm safe in assuming that this is the case for any of the professionals or business people who play this game. Can you imagine your surgeon telling you, "Hey, I'm just feelin' it. Like, dude, you know I really can't put it in words because I'm just goin' with the flow once I make the incision in your skull. Now just put on this mask, inhale and start counting backwards from one hundred."

Now admittedly that's an extreme example. But the fact remains that thinking got us where we are and it's not that easy to turn off the switch. Now the golf guru response to this would be to suggest that the objective really is to change how we think.

All right, let's talk about that.

We're all familiar with the pre-shot routine ritual in which we visualize the shot we want to hit. The problem that a lot of us have with this reminds me of something I once read about a tribe in the Andes called the Aymara. Now when we talk about past and future in spatial terms, we talk about the future as something in front of us and the past as something behind us.

The Aymara see it completely reversed. And I think they make a pretty good case. Their concept is that the past is what you know, and since it is known it is like anything else you can see: it lies in front of you. What you can't see, and is therefore unknown, are all the things in back of you. That's the future. So the Aymara will gesture ahead of them when remembering things and backward when discussing the future.

Now the author of this article said that this made the Aymara different from almost everyone else in the world. I think this only proves that the writer was not a golfer, because I think we tend to become Aymara as we contemplate a shot.

What we see in our mind's eye at that moment is often a resume, as it were, of our record with that particular shot. And as with any resume, there is an emphasis on the most recent experience. This can be a challenge when what fans out in front of us is an instant montage of ugly Kodak moments: shanks, chunks, skulls, hooks, slices or whatever misshapen shot we've been crafting recently out of this situation. This is the basis for that familiar predicament known as The Shot I'm Not Hitting Well These Days. The fact that you've hit it well at other times can feel about as relevant as your undergraduate major as you psych yourself up to try it again.

At this point the golf guru would insist that I've completely missed the point. For example, Dr. Bob Rotella says that great athletes create their own reality. They tell themselves they can pull off a shot and even if they don't, it doesn't bother them. Well, that's great

Bob, but when did we change the topic of conversation? I thought we were discussing me, not great athletes.

There's a word for a golfer like me who goes out and tries to create his own reality while playing: delusional. Besides, when it comes to thinking, not only do I find it hard to stop doing it, I like being right when I do it. I could tell myself that I'm going to pure the shot but there's part of me that's more comfortable looking at the stats and predicting some other outcome. It's like having a little bookie inside me who's quoting odds every time I address the ball. And it seems like I'm never playing with the house's money.

And as for playing without a conscious thought, well that almost seems scary. When my mind goes blank, that just what it does. It goes blank. It's not a moment of enlightenment. It's more like a brownout. There's a dip in power production and my body just decides that it only has enough juice for essential functions and my mind just doesn't qualify. But still this notion of playing without a conscious thought really isn't asking a lot if you consider that in an average round you spend only about three minutes swinging a club and striking the ball in some manner. Three minutes, that's all we're asking. Just don't think for three minutes. You can do it. After all you spent your adolescence doing it for months at a time.

But in the end I guess the bottom line about thinking and golf is that the Bobby Jones quote is essentially correct, it's just that the Aymara golfer in us sees it the other way around, as follows:

"When I have no swing thoughts I can play like Bobby Jones. If I have one, maybe I'll have a good shot. But if I have two thoughts then I can play like Paul Staley."

CHAPTER 13

GOLF AND THE MIND

We've all heard about the Zone, right? It's the antithesis of a place that's littered with swing thoughts. It's that magical place beyond space and time where everything just clicks. Descriptions of it have always reminded me of those montage sequences in a movie, the part where the guy and the girl start to fall in love. There are shots of them riding bikes together, feeding each other strawberries or laughing when one of them tries on a funny hat in a thrift store. Except that in the Zone, it's long approach shots checking up next to the pin, forty-foot snaking putts rattling into the cup and magnificent drives coming to rest in the middle of the fairway,

At least that's what I've been told. For me the Zone is that hot new restaurant where I can't get a reservation. It's the trendy night-club where I can't get past the velvet rope. On those occasions when I have managed to slip past the doorman somehow the bouncers always find me, and before I know it I'm back out on the sidewalk.

It's not that I don't believe in the Zone. In fact I think there are as many zones as there are golfers, because one man's zone is another man's purgatory. Let's say for the sake of argument that I shoot 76 not once, not twice, but three times in a row. I can assure you there would be a bounce to my step and I'd be talking some trash, at least until the NCGA caught up with me the next month. Tiger does the same thing and he's thinking that staying home with the new girlfriend doesn't seem like such a bad idea, and he's having his agent look into whether he can get any endorsements as a retired disgraced golfer.

As I said before, the problem with the Zone isn't so much finding it as staying there. We tell ourselves a lot of crazy stuff out there on the golf course. People who are supremely accomplished in their professional lives can be heard characterizing themselves as pathetic, stupid, incompetent and just plain idiotic, and that's just the sanitized list. But nothing is quite as insidious as the evidently prevalent notion among golfers that things have to average out. A string of good shots is bound to be followed by something less pleasant. A birdie is nice, but in the end it's just a set up for humiliation on the next hole.

(Interestingly. I don't think that people believe as strongly in the opposite assertion that poor shots must be followed at some point in the round by good ones. I had a playing partner for a while who held this belief despite what I thought was pretty overwhelming evidence to the contrary. I'm telling you, he lost so many presses he became a human ATM.)

So what's going on here? I think the problem is that we all have an image in our heads of what kind of golfer we are. When we start doing better we're convinced that we're going to have one of those moments like Wile E. Coyote in the Road Runner cartoons when he realizes that he's run way past the edge of the cliff and has nothing but air between his feet and the canyon floor thousands of feet below.

Look, it's kind of impossible not to be aware of how you're playing. The paradox of performing well and yet remaining detached from that performance is one of the great challenges in any sport, particularly golf. I'm always reminded of a post-game interview with a pitcher who was asked when he became aware that he was pitching a no-hitter, to which he responded, "It's not that hard a thing to keep track of."

How can we not think about how we're playing? It's not like we're out there playing jai alai. We've got way too much time to think about it. In fact, the actual act of hitting a golf ball in a round of golf is a lot like sex in marriage: there are long intervals between events and it's over pretty quickly. Back in the 17th century the French philosopher Descartes wrote, "I think therefore I am." The golfer corollary to this would be "I think therefore I suck," or for those who prefer the original Latin: Cogito ergo suck.

GOLF AND THE DALAI LAMA

The concept of the Zone and performance with the absence of thought reminds me of an interview with the Dalai Lama, part of which went as follows:

Q: You've called yourself a "semi-retired Dalai Lama." When people in America retire, they often take up games like golf. What does a semi-retired Dalai Lama do?

A: In a way I play golf in my interior life. For four hours every morning I do meditation. The meditation I practice is not just to sit there in thoughtlessness. I analyze. It's like brainstorming sessions. So within the brain you see a kind of competition taking place between the various poles of emotions. (He laughs.) In a sense this is more fun than golf.

Q: Who wins the competition?

A: Sometimes negative emotions win. Sometimes positive emotions win.

First off, what about the four-hour thing? Doesn't that strike you as a little eerie? Here's the biggest guy in Buddhism claiming to play golf in his "interior life" and he devotes the amount of time that playing 18 real holes should require. Is this just a coincidence, or an expression of some fundamental law of the universe? Just as 90 feet appears to be "just right" for baseball as the distance from home plate to first base, is four hours the right interval of time for a true test of one's ability to engage in relaxed concentration?

Or is His Holiness just playing with us since he's spent enough time with celebrities and Hollywood types to know that a round of real golf should take four hours? And, finally, for all we know he could be slipping away in the afternoon to play the physical version of the game. He kind of gives himself away when he says that his version is more fun than golf. How does he know if he hasn't played? And besides, what does he know from fun? Now going out on a cold wet morning and missing four three-foot putts and losing $40 in the process, that's what I call fun!

Now he may be playing a different game than the rest of us, but I'm going to go out on a limb here and bet that he's pretty good at it. In fact I bet he's better than scratch. And doesn't it make you happy when you see somebody who's picked the right profession? In a world where there are too many bored lawyers and disillusioned doctors here's a guy in his seventies who's clearly in the right line of work. But then again, according to the precepts of his religion he is the reincarnation of an earlier Dalai Lama, so maybe I shouldn't be that impressed. If my whole life was a mulligan I'd be a lot more relaxed about everything too.

For me the most interesting part is his answer to the question of who wins the competition: "Sometimes negative emotions win, sometimes positive emotions win." Because it is this battle between positive and negative emotions that provide the drama in that unscripted part of our pre-shot routine, what I'll call The Pause.

This is the interval right before you start your takeaway. For some players, and not coincidentally most of the better ones, this pause is almost imperceptible. For others it is a countdown that seems to start at a number higher, sometimes much higher, than ten.

The Pause is the ultimate It's All In Your Head moment. This is when we try to subdue the negative and summon the positive. As we contemplate the shot we find ourselves wanting nothing more than the calm focused mind of someone who meditates for a living. But it's not always like that, is it? Real relaxation can't be summoned instantly, or at least not for me. Breathing deeply doesn't work like a breath mint. It's more like a room freshener: you can still smell the stench of stress just below that veneer of lavender or citrus.

I'd love to have a mind as placid as the still surface of a pond in a Zen painting, but in reality my mind is more like a lava lamp, viscous and undulating with things that bubble to the surface. When contemplating yet another difficult shot around the green, I have at times felt that my mental pre-shot routine consists of playing an interior version of Whack-a-Mole, as every possible bad shot pops its head up to taunt me: "Hey Paul, how about chunking it into the bunker?" WHACK! "Hey, what about me, the skulled shot across the green?" WHACK! "Hey loser, what about getting cute, decelerating and advancing the ball a mere ten inches?" WHACK!

Other times the turmoil is subtler. When it comes to tee shots I can find myself going through a process that feels somewhat political, a sort of Tee Shot by Committee. Inevitably the Guy Who Wants to Crush It carries the day on at least a few holes in a performance that feels like a role for Mel Gibson or John Belushi: "If we don't swing hard now, when will we? NOW is the time! We've been straight off the tee all round and this is the number three handicap hole. Come on let's rip it!! Rip it!!!" And this leads, if not on the very next hole then soon after, to a legislative victory by the Swing Easy Party who are swept back into office on a surge of voter anger over lost golf balls and scores well above par.

One of the problems with all this mental back and forth is that I'm often just taking inventory of things I don't want to do, not identifying what it is I want to accomplish. Now I think it can be safely said that nothing great in this world ever began with the intention of wanting merely not to screw up. Obviously I wasn't there, but something tells me that when the block of marble that became Michelangelo's David arrived in the great man's studio he didn't approach it, hammer and chisel in hand, saying to himself, "Boy I hope this doesn't suck too much."

So, it would appear that the solution is to banish the boogiemen and then select the shot you want, right? Not really, because that could take a lot of time. And the problem with this is that, based on personal experience and observation, the longer The Pause, the lousier the shot. I've come to see The Long Pause as the equivalent of holding an elevator door open. You want to hit a great shot, don't you? You want to take it all the way to the penthouse, so to speak. So what are you doing holding the door open so all these other people can get on? Look here's that creepy guy from accounting that you're convinced is a pedophile, and look out, here's some weird dude from IT, and great, here's another bike messenger. Nope, the longer you wait, the weirder and more crowded it gets in there.

And deciding that you've had enough already with the golf blooper highlight reel and just starting your backswing doesn't always work too well. My mind may be nimble but it doesn't appear capable of making that kind of seamless transition. It's not like channel surfing. In addition to being a procrastinator I am by nature a hesitator. If procrastination describes a habit of putting things off over the span of days, weeks or even longer, then hesitation is its cousin on the micro-scale of the moment to moment. I am not by nature a "There's no time like the present" type guy. There is almost always another time, in fact by definition there is always going to be another time: just wait and it will arrive, to be followed in due course by another set of possible moments, all of them a little ways into the future and by my reckoning likely to be more propitious than the present one, ad infinitum. And so it is that I can become almost paralyzed over the shot, locked at address like a statute. In these situations the impulse to just get the goddamn process started begins with the thought, "Wow this is taking too long," and that in turn leads to a swing a description of which would not include the word 'tempo'. These are the occasions that get ugly for my golf balls, because this is when they get stabbed, not stroked.

The challenge of clearing one's mind before hitting the ball became a particularly interesting one for me since I have a daily meditation practice. Now in theory you'd think that would have helped me but no, it was actually quite the opposite. Maybe I'm not sitting long enough because I don't tend to get to any state of relaxation or heightened consciousness when I'm meditating. Instead it's more like a ten-minute check in to see what's rattling through my skull that morning. So I've come to view it as a quick trip through the multiplex inside my head. There's everything from G rated to X, a lot of sequels, nothing with subtitles but a whole lot of subtext. The best I can say about my practice is that I have learned to treat my thoughts like my wife handles clothing when she's shopping. She touches the fabric, pulling the garment slightly out from the rack, and then, in the vast majority of cases, she lets it go. So, in turn, I have learned to touch and then let go, touch the thought and let it go. If it's the lead story of the day it will come right back and then I have to touch and let go again and again.

So when it came to clearing my mind I have had to recognize that my meditation practice had only succeeded in developing a better set of internal antennae and a looser grip on the thoughts that flash through my brain. The problem when it came to golf was that when I treated the pre-shot routine as a meditative exercise my mind would view it as just another opportunity to see what was bubbling about in my head. What I needed to do instead was apply a variation of that venerable public service announcement: don't think and drive.

Of course there are the other times, when your visualization of the shot is so vivid that in your mind you can see not only what the result looks like but sense the physical feeling of executing it. Those are the times that as you pause over the ball, your mind says, "Let's do it." That's a lot different than "Let's get this over with." And when it comes to our game, that's the difference between positive and negative emotions.

THE POST-SHOT ROUTINE

The role of the mind in our golf games underscores the importance of something that is rarely discussed in the literature: a good post-shot routine. And by that I mean something other than a fist pump or a tip of the cap, you know, something you're going to use more often. Because, let's face it, almost every time you address the ball for a shot requiring a full swing the result is going to be less than perfect. That's why holes in one and eagles are such causes for celebration. The overwhelming odds are that the best you can aspire to is good enough and that a distressingly large number of times you will have a result that falls short of expectation. So how to handle this?

I once read that if you mishit a shot you should immediately repeat the swing and imagine that you pured it. This is supposed to reinforce the positive and keep the negative at bay. I never really tried it because I was worried that by the end of the round I would be in the grip of the sort of psychosis that afflicts abused children who can become seriously detached from reality because of repeatedly denying what happened and trying to replace it with what they wish had happened.

The real problem is that we have an instinctive post-shot routine that is a partial re-enactment of the five stages of grief as outlined by Elisabeth Kubler-Ross: denial, anger, bargaining, depression and acceptance. It's partial because denial isn't really part of the post-shot routine as much as it is the part of our pre-shot routine that helps set the stage for the next four stages of grief. Denial is the active ingredient in club or shot selections that are clearly based on a willful overestimation of our skills: "Oh well, since I'm between clubs the thing to do here is muscle up on a six-iron, that usually works well," or "Yeah, the ball's above my feet but I can still fade it around those trees." And in reality, as much as we try, denial can't be part of our post-shot routine because as quick as our minds are they aren't that fast. We sense immediately that our effort was less than textbook quality.

Our instinctive post-shot routine is also partial because we often never get to the final and fifth stage, acceptance. Therein lies the final irony: the good doctor's blueprint actually defines an appropriate process for dealing with our shots. But like our follow-throughs, we just don't finish properly. Let's take a closer look.

The sound track that we provide during a round demonstrates how quickly we move from stage two, anger, to stage three, bargaining. Our brains, which were complicit in the bad swing (I mean really, what were we thinking about at the time?) instantly register disgust with the result with a grunt or a profanity that is followed almost instantly by shouted instructions to the ball, as we try futilely to negotiate with a dimpled little sphere that has no ears.

But once the ball that you pushed to the right fails somehow to draw, or the wedge shot that you thinned ignores your pleas to "sit", the reality of your situation sets in. Now you get to move to stage four, depression. Now it's time to cue up the old favorites that comprise your Golf Mix Tape, timeless classics like "Why Am I Such a Headcase?" and "Why The Fuck Can't I Hit A Simple Eight-Iron?" And here is the real problem: it's only a short time interval between your leaving the scene of the crime and arriving at the next resting place for your poor golf ball and the necessity of moving to the final stage, acceptance, wherein you have to accept that you have short-sided yourself in the bunker once again. But the music never really stops. It plays on in your head like the muzak in the mall, faint perhaps, but persistent.

And that's the problem. We may trudge into the bunker and strike the pose of somebody addressing the shot but our minds are still a little ways back up the road, stewing about the swing that got us in this predicament. Our minds will be pinballing between stages two and four: cursing our misfortune ("They should name this fuck-ing bunker after me"), bargaining with an indifferent clique of golf gods ("Just let me get out of here with bogey"), or mired in self-pity ("God I suck"). What's missing is that final stage, acceptance. And real acceptance combines an understanding of why things happened ("I came over the top") with a real recognition that what is done cannot be undone. You both diagnose and accept the verdict. Case closed: time to move on.

CHAPTER 14

GOLF AND RELIGION

Golf is a very precise game, some might argue unfairly so. One of the classic lines after teeing off and torquing the ball into the next fairway is to remark, "It's a game of inches." But there is more than a kernel of truth behind this sarcasm. Relative to the scale of our regular lives, the margin of error when your driver's clubface struck the ball wasn't all that great. It really was a matter of degrees and fractions, admittedly large ones, of an inch. But the results were horrible.

A problem that many of us face as golfers is that with the exception, I hope, of those of you who are surgeons, our lives are built on approximation. "What time do you want us over?" "Oh, around seven." "How long a flight is it?" "About three hours." Large investment decisions are made on the basis of pro formas, which is Latin for "I'm just guessing." We can always press the delete key. We can cut and paste. It doesn't have to be perfect.

But there's no place out on the golf course for "sort of" or "kind of." And nowhere is that more true than when putting. Bad putters can look like they're lagging four footers. The hole might as well be some distant constellation. It's out there somewhere and they just hope the satellite gets close.

Like it or not, putting is a critical, if not the critical part of the game. "Drive for show, blah, blah, blah." But unfortunately this fact has done a lot to undermine the image of our beloved sport. Consider the average *SportsCenter* broadcast and it's no wonder millions of people don't consider golfers athletes. There's some Billy Joe Bob impersonating a tumbleweed as his souped up Dodge cartwheels down some speedway in Alabama and we've got a linebacker beheading some wide receiver on a crossing pattern and some NBA players pulling off 360 degree tomahawk slam-dunks. But wait! Hold on to your seats, here's Kenny Perry rolling in a twelve-footer to win the Greater Raleigh Subaru Open. WOW!!!

Now we all know how difficult putting can be. But it just doesn't look like much to an outsider. It's not a complicated physical act, just one where the margin of error is so minute. And what happens when people confront such exacting judgment? Why they get religion of course. Events on the putting green take on aspects of worship and ritual. If you don't believe me, step back and think about what happens there.

First there's the finality of it all. Think of a round of golf as 18 little stories. As your group approaches the green, the particular story that hole represents, whether heroic masterpiece or comedic farce, is nearing its conclusion. Unless there's been some improbable event like an ace or a chip-in, it all gets decided on the putting green. It's time to tie up the loose ends and see what the final outcome will be. There is a definite "Dearly beloved we are gathered here today" type feel to it. This is it.

As in many religions most participants in this rite have their heads covered. Some hold metal objects up in their hands. Others squat down, peering at the contours of Mother Earth. It gets kind of ecumenical out there. At some point everybody turns to the hole as if it were Mecca. The small practice strokes look like genuflections. Guys confer in quiet voices as if they were off to the side of the bima at temple. And then everybody stands still and all conversation ceases as each supplicant takes his or her turn making an offering, each praying that the hole will accept it.

And most times the hole rejects it. As happens so often, prayers go unanswered. In the aftermath of this rejection things tend to get profane. No matter what their level of ability players don't behave well when confronted with the reality that Missed Putts Happen to Good People. If you're Tiger, you fall to your knees as if you had just been told that your mother had died. If you're one of my playing partners you become so despondent that you question out loud everything in your existence: your intelligence, your athletic ability, your body fat content, even your sexual orientation. The wailing and rendering of garments becomes almost Biblical.

And don't think for a minute that this is one of those occasions of loss when your friends are going to be there for you. Because in actuality, prayers have been answered: those of your opponents. Once again they have been delivered from losing a hole because of your pathetic inability to roll in a simple five footer. And your partner? He can't afford much more of this and is already thinking of any sort of plausible excuse for not being available for a game next week (as in going to temple or church, or better yet, both). You stand alone in your suffering. All that's left in this particular little tragedy is for somebody to say one of two things: either the charitable "That's good," or the more dismissive "Take it away." It's time to move on to the next story.

THE GOLF GODS

The exacting nature of putting and the quasi-religious response that it inspires in us brings us to a related topic. The debate over the separation of church and state has been a big topic through the ages. The separation of church and golf, not so much. So, since it doesn't appear to be a real hot button issue, I thought I'd dive right in. Let's take a look at what a blend of different religious traditions and golf would look like. You might discover that you're playing a brand of golf that's different from your professed creed. And hopefully, you may even come away having learned something about another faith.

But before beginning there is one observation I have to share: aside from the usual profane applications, I rarely hear a player during a round invoke the name of the singular, monotheistic entity that is the popular version in these parts. I've always found it interesting that it is much more common to hear somebody say that the golf gods, as in plural not singular, have intervened.

Several explanations for this come to mind. The first is that it is an indirect acknowledgement on our parts of the true cosmic insignificance of our golf game and that it borders on disrespect to think that the Being in Charge of Everything has the time or inclination to get involved in whether our second putt lips out or not. In certain respects it is an indication of respect for the divine. The decision not to petition the Almighty to get involved in our chosen form of recreation indicates an acknowledgement that doing so would constitute a grievous misuse of that majestic power. We appear to have decided that, as paradoxical as it seems, even omnipotence and omniscience have their limits and need to be applied judiciously.

Thus it could be that when we attribute certain events on the course to the golf gods and not God, singular and with a capital "G", we are simply acknowledging that the Big Guy is just a tad too busy to check in on whether we deserve to have our tee shot ricochet back onto the fairway or further into the trees. It boils down to a spiritual version of *He's Just Not That Into You.* He cares about you, but not enough to get involved in your golf game.

Or alternatively, it may be that having been raised in a monotheistic culture we are more comfortable attributing the random bounces and twists and turns of our golf balls to a set of gods. We were taught that the Big Guy doesn't do random. But if everything, including what takes place on the golf course happens for a reason that leads to an inevitable and uncomfortable conclusion, namely that He doesn't really care for us and frankly seems to enjoy seeing us suffer. And that is just too painful to accept. It's far better to resort to the sort of polytheistic scheme that can explain our setbacks as the result of the capricious whims of minor deities who just like to mess with us.

Polytheism may not be very good at moral clarity but it certainly is better at explaining bad outcomes. If there is one God and He/She is good then how do you explain all this bad stuff that happens? This is where a lot of young religious belief runs off the tracks. But if you have multiple gods then you can rationalize away all sorts of bad stuff: this god felt slighted so he decided to screw up somebody's business, or this goddess was jealous so she intervened in a dispute. If heaven is really some celestial version of MTV's *The Real World* with a bunch of bickering and conniving deities then the bad stuff that happens on the course is still frustrating but slightly more comprehensible.

The notion that the golf gods meddle with us gets a good amount of indirect support from the tendency of the various components of our game to behave quite differently from each other over the course of a round. This is the all too familiar experience of driving well but putting horribly, or vice versa, or any of a number of other possible combinations of the good, the bad and the ugly. It begins to feel like your golf game is governed by some committee up in the heavens where attendance is erratic and those who do show up tend to be cranky. And most of us would agree that the Chairman of the Board is the God of Putting and he is hardly ever in a good mood.

Or if you prefer a more psychologically oriented explanation, the invocation of the golf gods is just more evidence of the stress that the game inflicts on us. In this instance we are thrown back to a state of mind that is not only pre-scientific but pre-monotheistic as well. It harkens back to those days thousands of years ago when rather than being married to one God instead we were essentially dating a bunch of them. In order to get what we wanted, or ask forgiveness, we just made sure that we brought something nice along as a gift like flowers or a young animal.

But there's a problem here. Golf doesn't respond to sucking up. Sure you can spend money on equipment and lessons, but the only people who are guaranteed to be pleased by your largesse are the manufacturers and your pro. The game itself? It could care less. You may spend a lot of time with it but it is not your spouse and you can't buy yourself forgiveness, or if you're being pre-emptive, any slack, by giving it flowers or a bottle of perfume. But of course, this was the problem with all the traditions of sacrifice and offering that marked religious observance in days gone by: great business for the vendors outside the temple, not so good on ensuring the desired outcome. Golf just expresses the indifference the universe seems to have for so much that we do. It is this inflexible, unyielding and ulti-mately insensitive aspect of the game that contributes to the belief that something or Somebody has to be responsible. Otherwise we'd be left to conclude that we've taken up a sport that's fundamentally cruel and we don't want to go there. Of course we don't get too carried away with this notion that something is meddling with our game, otherwise we'd have golf horoscopes in the sports pages and we haven't seen that, at least not yet.

It also seems, based on the behavior of professional athletes, that God is simply not all that into golf anyway. Although he may get his props in an interview here and there, he certainly doesn't get the kind of recognition out on the course that He gets in other venues. If all the genuflecting and gazes and gestures to the heavens really are indications that Somebody Up There is watching then it seems pretty clear that the Big Guy is into football and baseball in a big way but everything else really doesn't do it for Him. It appears that

He enjoys all the stuff that the rest of us like, such as home runs and touchdowns; in other words he's a big fan of ESPN's *SporsCenter*. I'm sure He appreciates the value of good defense but somehow the word has gotten out that He doesn't expect credit for a good tackle quite as much as He likes sharing the glory for an acrobatic touchdown catch or a three-run home run. But nobody, not even the big believers on the Tour, drop to their knees or genuflect after the bunker shot holes out or the twisting thirty-footer rattles into the cup for birdie and the outright lead.

But even if He really isn't paying attention, because let's say the Red Sox and the Yankees are on ESPN yet again, there can still be a quasi-religious feeling to what happens out on the course. I'm thinking of those instances of unexpected good play when you feel like you're in one of those paintings by the old masters in which shafts of light break through the clouds to illuminate the saint as he or she goes about doing whatever saintly activity is being portrayed. It's a wonderful feeling, but unlike the painting, it doesn't last.

THE SEPARATION OF CHURCH AND GOLF

So let's get back to our original premise, the separation, or lack thereof, between golf and religion. There is no better way to examine this neglected topic than a catalogue of the different combinations of religious belief and golf. For example, Jewish golf is all about suffering, and no book of the Old Testament expresses this better than the Book of Job. As with most golf outings it begins with a bet. God says to Satan, "Hey check out my man, Job, there's a dude that's totally down with me." To which Satan responds, "Oh yeah? Well, let's see what happens when you take away all his possessions and his family and everything he loves. We'll see how fond he is of you then, Big Guy." And so the bet is on.

So Job winds up losing everything. You think you've had some bad days? Grab the Old Testament some time and check out the first couple chapters of the Book of Job. That's a run of bad luck.

So, understandably, Job flips out. He has three friends (i.e. the rest of his foursome) and they spend a lot of time either giving him a pep talk or the tough love treatment. By the sixth chapter he's begging for tips: "Teach me and I will be silent; make me understand how I have gone wrong." Finally in the 38th chapter, God makes an appearance and he delivers the big smack down. Basically He asks Job where he gets the nerve to complain. "Did you create the universe?" he asks and just to underscore how amazing He is, He proceeds to catalogue everything he created all the way down to specific mammals. It's pretty pedantic stuff and it's easy to imagine Job saying to himself, "Okay, I get it; you don't have to go all the way down the food chain."

In the end the advice that God delivers is the following, and I quote: "Gird up your loins like a man." That's right, the moral of the story is "Sack up." Life's tough so stop bitching about it. Job repents and God gives him everything back and then some.

So what, you might ask, does any of this have to do with golf, to which I would have to respond, "Good question." But since I brought up the whole thing I am somewhat obligated to make some sort of connection and this is the best I can do: the essence of Jewish golf, as relayed in the story of Job, is that everything can be fine, just hunky dory and then, oy, you lose your swing, the putts don't drop, it all starts to slip away and you're thinking to yourself, this is supposed to be fun, why am I so upset? My doctor told me it would be good for me, get me out in the fresh air, but who knew? This is so stressful, for this aggravation I pay money? I know, I know, I shouldn't complain, there are people far worse off than myself and if anything bad should happen to me, God forbid, I would miss my friends....

As for Christian golf, my Jewish friends' understanding of Christianity has often underwhelmed me. To many of them the religion just looks like a collection of fairy tales with anti-Semitic ramifications. From their perspective while the Old Testament may have its share of over the top special effects, such as oceans that separate so that people can walk through them or bushes that burn and talk at the same time, that's all they are, special effects. The New Testament on the other hand has a plot line that requires you to believe a whole lot of weird stuff like virgins who give birth and dead bodies that just get up and keep on going.

So allow me to define some terms for everybody. First of all you have your two basic types, Protestant and Catholic. Now the Protestant side is your Baskin-Robbins of religion: you can choose from a wide variety of flavors as long as you understand that they're all made from the same basic materials. And differentiating between some denominations is a bit like knowing the difference between Double Mint Chocolate Chip and Mint Swirl Chocolate Chip. And in fact, if pressed to explain this difference most Mint Swirl Chocolate Chip eaters will confess that their choice really wasn't a choice at all but simply a question of what flavor their parents ate.

So first off, I have some good news. As proof that God really is merciful, for Christian golfers there are only nine commandments. He recognized that as a golfer and a human being you could score perfectly on idolatry and adultery and all that other stuff but that there was absolutely no way you could avoid taking His name in vain. Plus, nine's an appropriate number, don't you think?

But, perhaps appropriately, Christian golf is also the realm of the eerie coincidence of which I have two examples. The first involves a feeling that I'm sure that many of you have had, namely the sense that no matter what you do, no matter how many lessons you take or how much you spend on equipment, you will just go on being basically the same sort of lousy of golfer you've always been. It's as if you were just fulfilling a fate for which you were pre-destined. You were just born to be a 19. Now here's the coincidence: the concept of pre-destination as an aspect of Christian philosophy was part of Calvinism, a particularly stern form of Protestantism that was prevalent in....Scotland. So the attitude that you can't do anything about your fate flourished in the same place as the game that leaves you feeling that you can't do anything about it. Maybe it's not a coincidence.

The second example involves a particular Catholic saint. Now saints can be a little confusing to the non-Catholic and for those of us not raised in the Church they only come into play as part of our tourist experience when we're trying to figure out what it is we're looking at in a fresco or stained glass window. It's best to think of them as playing the role that UPS or FedEx do in internet commerce. There is your prayer, or in the other case your online order, but you still need someone to act on your behalf, to deliver the goods as it were. This is what a saint does. What's particularly relevant to our discussion here is that saints have, among other things, a specialty or a particular cause with which they are identified and thus they have a symbol for that affiliation that artists back in the day could use as a way of identifying them for largely illiterate congregations. Which brings us to Saint Jude who is the patron saint of lost causes. Want to guess what his symbol is? It's a club. You can look it up.

Now I don't know what Hindu golf is all about but I suspect it involves a prayer of gratitude that as a mere mortal and not a god like Shiva, you don't have to worry about aligning eight arms when you swing the club. There's probably also a provision that says even if you totally suck at the game, if you're a good partner, don't cheat and pay your bets, you get to be reincarnated as a low handicapper next time around. Islamic golf? Again, my information is sketchy but I do understand that there are no Ladies days, no beer carts and lots of sand. And Mormon golf? In the old days, the couples tournaments were a logistical nightmare. And for all we know there could be a sect somewhere in Utah who believe that when Jesus came over here he introduced golf to the Native Americans, but then they screwed it all up by making it a team game where you passed the ball around and that's how lacrosse was born.

Buddhist golf seems like it has promise. There's all that meditating and emphasis on mental clarity. You're supposed to let go of things (ego, fear, anger, the club head) and you're supposed to be present in the moment. But there's one problem. According to what I've read, Buddhist golf is what Tiger started playing in 2010 and he didn't win a thing that year.

CHAPTER 15

GOLF AND PHILOSOPHY

So let's be honest with ourselves and admit that it's hard to elevate our games. But why let that hold us back? If you can't bring your game to the next level then elevate the context. If you're going to be frustrated by something the least you can do is make it less trivial. Sure Bob Rotella and the old geezer with the little red book are good instructors but it's still all about the little ball and the only slighter bigger hole in the ground. If you're going to feel lousy about something make it worthwhile, or at least make it sound like it has some import.

Among life's bigger irritations is being bothered by something and then realizing that the thing that's bugging you is something minor, because then not only do you still have your initial level of irritation but you now have the additional disheartening realization that you've let something trivial get to you. Of course you could at that moment simply dismiss this Thing but for most of us that never works; it just bounces back, hitting all the same sore spots once again.

So, if you can't shake it or don't feel like relegating your problem to the waste basket of the insignificant (because for the purposes of this discussion we are talking about your golf game and that does matter) then you have no choice but to make It a Big Deal. And if you're going to do that you're going to need to bring in the heavyweights. It's time to bring in some of the biggest names in Western philosophy to see what they have to say about the game of golf. Finally, the beauty of this approach, if done properly, is that by elevating the context you can justify your obsession. You're no longer perturbed by something as cosmically insignificant as your putting; instead you're engaged in an application of some the greatest thinking in the history of western civilization.

PLATO SAYS, "TAKE A LESSON"

Plato's allegory of the cave is probably the most famous image in all of philosophy. In fact as far as I'm concerned it's the only famous image in philosophy. I'm sure if you gave me a couple minutes and an internet connection I could come up with some others but the cave is still going to be numero uno.

Anyway, in *The Republic,* Plato writes about how Socrates and his posse are hanging out having one of their bull sessions and the topic of education comes up. Socrates tells his crew to imagine that humans are living in an underground cave-like dwelling. They have been there since childhood, chained and fettered so that they can only see straight in front of them. In back of them is a fire and between them and the fire is a constant flow of people passing back and forth, conversing or carrying various objects. All they can see of the world that goes about its business in back of them are the shadows cast on the wall in front of them.

And so, asks Socrates, don't you suppose that these people chained in place and seeing only those shadows would assume that was reality? (At which point somebody in the group like totally said "Oh dude that is so heavy!") Well then, continued Socrates, what do you think would happen if you released one of these unfortunates from his chains and turned him towards the light?

"Well," answered one, "he'd have a hard time seeing at first because the light was so strong," at which point Socrates probably made a mental note not to call on that guy again. "But wouldn't it also be the case," asked Socrates, "that he would think that the shadows were truer than the bright strange images he was seeing for the first time?" "Yes," they answered.

It goes on like this for a while, but I think you get the point. Education is the process of turning yourself around so that you can see things as they are, not the reflections or shadows that you see when you are trapped in ignorance.

And so you ask what does this have to do with golf? Well, when it comes to our swings we are definitely prisoners in the cave. In fact before the advent of video, we literally had to rely on our shadows if we wanted to see what was going on. On the practice range we can pause and check on certain things, but as one wag pointed out, if you look back at your hands at the top of your backswing the only thing you will know for sure is which hand is wearing a glove. There is no way for us to step outside ourselves and see what is actually happening when we swing the club.

So if Socrates and the guys were golfers they would have recognized the necessity of getting a lesson, particularly when things aren't going right. You certainly don't want to rely on the observations and guidance of your regular foursome because they too are prisoners of the cave.

Seneca says, "Stop whining"

When I was contributing monthly columns to my club newsletter about the mental challenges of the game I became the club's unofficial golf confessor. People would confide in me that they were considering the unthinkable: quitting. Giving up on golf. It had become too frustrating, too aggravating. The notion of a relaxing round of golf had become a cruel oxymoron.

One day one of these members, who had been particularly despondent, told me that he had come to a realization that had helped him: "The secret to golf," he said, "is low expectations."

Now it should be obvious by now that I'm not a big one for the positive self-affirmation but I would make one modification to his assessment. The secret is not low, but realistic expectations.

As we anticipate a round of golf many of us will think in terms of some final result, i.e. posting a score within some range (our handicap plus or minus, and definitely more likely on the plus side) or finally winning some money back from that sandbagging swindler you call a friend. But by thinking in terms of this aggregate or financial result we ignore the ingredients that go into this concoction we call a round of golf. For most of us the relationship between goal and execution will look like this:

We will aim for the middle of the fairway but only occasionally find it. We will pick out landing areas in the fairways and wind up looking for our balls in the rough. Our approach shots, instead of coming to rest on the green, will instead find one of the design features that the course architect installed to penalize errant shots. A significant percentage of our putts will never see the bottom of the cup, and if we are conceding putts there will only be a handful of our efforts that result in that sweet little rattling sound.

So even a cursory review of our usual game would tell us what to expect as we set out once again on a weekend morning. And yet we all experience and express, sometimes quite vocally, our profound disappointment when they happen. But come on, what did you expect? At the end of the day you're not surprised that you shot 87; that's what you're supposed to do, more or less. But when you were playing, when the strokes were being tallied, the rest of your foursome heard your shock and dismay when the ten-footer didn't drop or that out-to-in swing path propelled your tee shot into the trees on the right.

Way, way back in the day there were a group of philosophers whose focus was on how people reacted to events in their life. They were known as the Stoics. The mere fact that their name is now part of our vocabulary indicates how successful they were. During their heyday everybody on the A-list in Rome was into it. The adoption of their name as a common adjective indicates the strength of their brand, in the same way that google is now a verb.

But our boiled down definition of what it means to be stoic misses the greater relevance of this philosophy to the game of golf. There is more to being a Stoic than simply being a good chap and keeping a stiff upper lip and all that. It's a matter of having realistic expectations as to what the world, or if you prefer, a round of golf, will be like. As one commentator on Seneca, one of the most famous Stoic philosophers, puts it, "What makes us angry are dangerously optimistic notions about what the world and other people are like."

As further evidence that Seneca was really Harvey Penick in a toga, consider this summary of his philosophy: "We best endure those frustrations which we have prepared ourselves for and understand and are hurt most by those we least expected and cannot fathom. Philosophy must reconcile us to the true dimensions of reality, and so spare us, if not frustration itself, then at least its panoply of pernicious accompanying emotions." So, to translate this into our golf experience, we don't get as pissed off about not making par on the number one handicap hole as we do about skulling a chip shot. But if we were really going to apply this philosophy we would have to recognize that we skulled the chip because we hardly spend any time practicing our short game and thus the proper response is not anger but a recognition that unless we practice these shots we should expect to screw them up from time to time.

And if you need more evidence that Stoicism is the proper framework for reshaping your attitude consider possibly the most irritating occurrence in the game: the lip out. I can't think of anything that better expresses the tendency of golf to violate our sense of what the ground rules of existence should be. Yeah, okay, maybe the ball was struck just a hair too firmly or just a centimeter off line, but wasn't that still good enough? I mean it was really, really close to being just right wasn't it?

But as the ball spins back away from the hole our outrage and disappointment can overwhelm us. But compare our reactions to this sort of event with how a professional handles it. When it's one of us the cursing and wailing and rendering of garments can be quite a spectacle. I had a playing partner say once, as The Ball That Should Have Gone In became instead The Ball That Spun Out, that he wanted to snap his putter in two and drive the shaft into his heart. The professional, on the other hand, will merely grimace ever so slightly or look away in disgust. On those rare occasions when a pro does start to lose it you can bet that the commentators in the booth will be all over him to get his act together. I remember Jeff Overton reacting to a lip-out one Sunday in a way that was positively mild compared to the histrionics I've seen in my foursome, and the broadcast guys were acting like he had pulled out a gun and was about to pistol whip his caddy.

IS LIFE MATCH PLAY OR MEDAL PLAY?

The observation that golf is like life is fairly commonplace. The idea is that the lessons learned on the course such as honesty and integrity can be applied to life in general. But if you reverse the sentence and assert that life is like golf you open up the door to a host of intriguing philosophical questions, such as the following: is life match play or medal play?

In other words, in our lives are we playing a game in which our performance is measured against some inflexible standard and we are but one competitor in a large field, or is our life a series of little competitions in which we take on one issue or one competitor at a time?

Or to rephrase it, does everything you do matter in some sort of permanent way because life is a continuous tally of the good and the bad, or do things matter only insofar as they affect a particular phase of your life and once that's over, it's over? In other words, yeah you chunked that seven-iron on the ninth hole but the clod you're playing launched his drive into the trees and then three-putted. Your hole. What seven-iron?

I'm not suggesting that there is a right or a wrong answer here. How we answer the question at any particular time could easily vary depending on how the game of life is going for us. When things are tough it is tempting to seek refuge in the comfort of relative performance, as in "Hey, I may not be doing all that well but I'm better off than that guy." Of course this attitude can lead to a sort of sleazy relativism in which there is always somebody who provides an appropriately low bar of comparison. One can imagine the following locker room conversation after a Morality Match Play event at Relativist Springs Golf Club:

"Hey, how'd your match go?"

"Great. Won 8 and 7."

"Whoa! Who'd you play?"

"This new member, Adolf Hitler."

"Don't know him."

"Short guy, bad haircut, weird moustache."

"Oh him. I've heard he doesn't have much of a game."

"Yeah, well he did win a hole. He is a vegetarian, you know."

"Ah, so at least he's kind to animals?"

"Nah, I think he hates plants."

Life as match play means that there is a built-in reset button in the competition. Yes, you just triple-bogeyed a hole but the damage is a mere one point. There is no undoing what has been done but you have not set yourself back three strokes and face the task of clawing your way back. You're down one more point and you could easily win that point back on the very next hole. In a match play world every day is the first day of the rest of your life. In a medal play world every day is another scorecard added to a really big pile of them.

At first glance all religions and ethical systems are medal play. In one popular version there are sins and there are good deeds, and admission to the Big Country Club in the Sky is a matter of how you did relative to par. But upon closer examination this idea of religion being medal play is not such a foregone conclusion. Let's not forget that the version of match play favored by most of us involves the option of calling for a press. Do well on the press and you can offset the effect of your previous poor play. And so, if you think about it, what are confession and penance or Yom Kippur or any other form of atonement if not a form of spiritual press? In both cases your debts and sins are erased. So it's not so obvious, is it?

Self-improvement regimes such as dieting are definitely medal play: calories in versus calories out. Some destructive habits such as binge and purge have more of a match play feel to them. Commuting to work is medal play, but once you get there work often has the flavor of match play.

So we could also conceive of life as akin to the PGA Tour Calendar, in which there are both medal and match play competition. Money matters are definitely medal play; your closing balance is your opening balance the next day. How you're doing is a matter of addition and subtraction in which every dollar counts. Love? Well, as always that's more complicated. Dating is definitely more like the driving range: everything is longer and straighter there. People seem more pleased with how they're doing and they hold out hope for what lies ahead.

Marriage? Well I'm going to go out on a limb and suggest the following: since most guys I know are screw-ups in some way or another there is going to be a difference of opinion on this question within most households. Wives are definitely medal play: they're keeping score and the tally goes back to the very beginning. It all counts. Husbands? Definitely match play: "Hey, I'm sorry. Can we just move on?"

How we answer this question also depends on old we are. When we are young and in school life definitely feels like medal play. Academics, and in particular the process of applying to college, are definitely medal competition. Your standing is a largely a function of numbers (GPA, SAT scores) and you are competing against a field of thousands. Want to get into Stanford? Well those Cs in biology and chemistry look a lot like triple bogeys.

Once we enter our professional lives though things begin to feel more like match play. It may not be head-to-head competition so much as advancing, or not, through a series of brackets: applying to be an associate, then going for partner, and then senior partner and so forth. Office politics? Definitely match play.

The concept of our professional lives as match play raises yet another, and potentially deflating consideration: to what extent are our successes the result of somebody else's failure and not so much the fruit of excellent performance on our part? Let's be honest here.

How often is there extra currency in your wallet after a match not because you were so awesome but because your opponent failed to play to his handicap? And back at the office, what deals or cases are won because somebody else screwed up, or simply wasn't as good in that instance as they could have been? As Woody Allen said, 80% of success is showing up.

CHAPTER 16

GOLF, POLITICS AND PSYCHOLOGY

But what if we took yet another perspective on the game? What if we imagined what kind of golfer some of the great figures of the arts, literature and history would have been.

Historians trace the origins of golf back to mid-15th century Scotland. Now this raises a number of interesting questions. First, there were bound to be implications for marital life even back then. It's one thing to get home late from a game that's well established and quite another to attribute your tardy return to a game that hasn't really been invented yet. In fact I think that students of Scottish history and culture have it all wrong and the adoption of the kilt as a form of male garb came after, not before, the invention of golf. I think the conversation went something like this: "Aye, Seamus, if ye'll have me believing that ye've been knocking a wee ball aboot the moors I've a bargin for ye. Ye can play this game ye fancy so if ye'll wear this wee tartan skirt I've been knittin." And thus the kilt, rather than an ancient predecessor to golf, is another example of how men will do just about anything to play the game.

Another admittedly obvious implication of the time and place of golf's birth is that millions of human beings never had a chance to play the game. You could have been a Pharaoh or a Pope, Genghis Khan or Leonardo da Vinci, and you never had a chance to play the greatest game ever invented. This is clearly a tragedy of monumental proportions.

But as Shivas Irons said in *Golf in the Kingdom*, golf is a mirror into the soul. A few years back a guy by the name of Franklin Foer wrote a great book on soccer and politics titled *How Soccer Explains the World*. This is more an example of How Golf Explains You. What we know about famous historical or literary figures should give us a pretty good idea of what their golf game would have been like. And so, in roughly chronological order, here are some answers to one of the great questions of historical analysis: "What kind of golfer would he have been?"

Moses: Obviously he would be a stickler for the rules and actually could be pretty tedious about insisting that he helped introduce them. Given that he took 40 years to get from Egypt to the Promised Land you definitely wouldn't want to get stuck playing in back of his foursome.

Job: Definitely a player. Anybody with that capacity for suffering was meant to be a golfer. Known to complain about his misfortunes though.

Jesus: Like most guys who are sons of the boss he would have lots of time to hang around the club and work on his game. It goes without saying that he'd have an awesome short game. If you can save souls, you can certainly save par. And when you have a guy who can multiply fishes and loaves like that, why have anybody else run your tournament committee? On the other hand this ability to walk on water would be useful only if he could get his golf balls to float.

Joan of Arc: The Michelle Wie of her time: not afraid to take on the guys, but a tendency to go down in flames at crunch time.

Henry VIII: What's a second marriage but another kind of mulligan? This guy had six wives so you can be sure that there would be a lot of "do-overs" in a round with him. And don't imagine for one second that you could actually stop him from hitting another ball anytime he thought that was a good idea. He wasn't exactly nice to people who got in his way.

Marquis de Sade: Definitely a scratch player. In certain respects the perfect opponent: not only would he have to give you strokes, he'd be happy to do so.

Louis XVIII and Marie Antoinette: They'd always be available for tournaments and parties. But the wigs would be a real problem on windy days, and let's face it: people who lose their heads aren't going to be winning any couples tournaments.

Hamlet: Without a doubt he would be the slowest player out there. To chip or not to chip? Driver or three-wood? It would be agony. On top of that there would be all this morbid talk about his dead caddy Yorick. By the back nine you would be yelling at him,

"Hey Hammie, put the skull back in the bag. You're freaking me out with that thing."

Beethoven: Only good for nine, but boy could he talk about how well he played the fifth and the ninth. "They were masterpieces, I tell you, masterpieces."

Thomas Jefferson: Probably not a great golfer, but he'd design your clubhouse and your course, oversee the landscaping and select all the wines. You'd have to watch him around the staff though.

Mozart: An extremely good junior golfer and not shy about letting you know that. "Really, Wolfie, that's just great. You got your first birdie when you were three years old? And you were breaking par by the time you were seven? Hey, thanks for reminding me and be sure and tell me again next time we play."

Hitler: No surprises here: a thoroughly despicable, ill-tempered maniac. And besides, he couldn't get out of a bunker to save his life.

FDR: I don't know, maybe he did play before polio struck him down. But, regardless, he belongs in this list because he gave us one of the best pieces of golf advice ever: "All we have to fear is fear itself."

GOLF AND POLITICS

But instead of just wondering what kind of golfer a famous person might have been, let's also consider what kind of person great golfers are.

Now it's fairly well known that professional golfers are a pretty conservative bunch. Some observers attribute this to the economic context of the game. It is after all the favored sport of business tycoons and the professional season is a series of tournaments sponsored by large corporations that usually feature a pro-am event in which successful business types get to play with the big boys. But the theory that immersion in the world of Big Money turns golfers conservative makes them sound, if not whorish than at least somewhat canine: throw them some endorsements and a little prize money and they'll just love you. "Yeah, who's a good golfer? Yeah, yeah, yes you are! That's a good boy, that's a good golfer. Who loves his corporate sponsor? Yeah, good boy."

I think it's fair to say that there's more than a little pre-selection going on here. Golf doesn't make conservatives as much as it attracts them. It's not like it's any big secret that at its highest level the game is played at exclusive locations and is essentially solitary; we're not talking about some Masonic ritual that's revealed only when you're allowed inside the temple. Remember this is a sport where teamwork consists of helping your partner read a putt. The professional golfer is a modern version of the medieval knight who jousts in front of nobility with only his faithful valet at his side. He does not see himself as a part in some greater whole: he is not the pulling guard on a running play or the defensive specialist who comes off the bench late in the game. He is there to do everything himself and he does it solely for the benefit of his family and retinue of agents, coaches and sponsors.

Professional athletes in team sports may be extravagantly paid but they are, in the end, no different than Wall Street bankers: employees of corporations where people are overly compensated for doing things that have little or no redeeming social value. Golfers, on the other hand, are the ultimate independent entrepreneurs, managing a small business: their golf game. There is corporate affiliation, of course, but this is a matter not of employment but advertising, as companies bid to place little billboards, as it were, on the body of the golfer, the preferred locations being the forehead and above his or her left nipple.

Viewed from this perspective it shouldn't be a surprise that golfers are mainly a conservative lot. You would expect as much from any group of independent businesspeople who have embraced and succeeded in ventures that require such a high degree of self-reliance. If strokes are viewed as a form of expenditure, then the winner will be the competitor whose cost of production is the lowest. Professional golfers therefore will behave like any entrepreneur whose goal is ever increasing levels of efficiency. Their prescription for any social problem would be the application of what has worked for them: independence, self-discipline and hard work. Such a philosophy doesn't allow a lot of room for government programs or subsidies or regulation.

And yet as true as any of this may be, I still think we can go deeper. After all, any argument that makes political affiliation a function of economic identity, is just so, dare I say it, Marxist. Perhaps there is such a thing as an inherently conservative brain and that mind is better suited for golf than the more left-wing version.

This really shouldn't strike us as a strange notion. Of course a brain that believes that lowering taxes won't increase government deficits is ideally designed for a game that involves contradictory notions such as the necessity of hitting down on the ball in order to make it go up. And, after all, a game that rewards a mind that strives for consistency will never be one that is kind to one that embraces diversity. Finally, the conservative mind is one that believes that if you do the right thing, good outcomes will result, whereas the liberal version jumps immediately to constructing that outcome. In other words, just as a conservative politician has faith that the market left to its own devices will benefit all participants, the good golfer has faith that a well-rehearsed and well-executed swing will produce a good outcome. On the other side of the aisle, the liberal mind sees people in need and moves immediately to some form of intervention, and on the golf course a similar impulse leads to the tinkering and mid-course adjustments that may or may not achieve the intended result. You start guiding the club or the putter instead of simply trusting that following certain principles will produce success.

Good golf is an orderly process often played in locations where there are decades, if not centuries, of tradition. The champion performer is the one who, under extraordinary pressure, is the most consistent, which is just another way of saying the one whose swing changes the least in the heat of competition. This is classic, old school conservatism, not the libertarian "Don't Tread on Me" version that is popular these days in the United States. This is the conservatism of Burke not Beck. This is respect, even reverence, for doing the same things the same way no matter what, and golf, perhaps more than any other game, is going to reward that frame of mind.

IT's ALL IN YOUR HEAD

So here we are again, in the small bit of real estate above your neck. Even the politics of golf are only a manifestation of the psychology of the game. The question of how one's state of mind affects one's state of play brings to mind the observation of English psychologist

Adam Phillips who once said that we'd like our brains to function like benign dictatorships. It would be nice to know that somebody is in charge and additionally comforting if we could be sure that entity had our better interests in mind.

And yet we find ourselves behaving in ways that completely belie that desire, and nothing better illustrates this than our attitude towards, and our actual application of, course management. (Before beginning, however, it bears mention that course management is yet another of those inherently misleading terms. After all, you're not managing the course, that's the job of the guys with the agronomy degrees who oversee the maintenance crew and who always seem to be punching and sanding the greens just when you're getting used to them. No, you're managing yourself, or trying to.)

First, as far as our attitude about course management, the relative popularity of professional players speaks volumes on the issue. We like the dashing and the reckless. We love Phil and we loved Seve (except when he was playing against our guys in the Ryder Cup). Zach Johnson, who laid up on the par-fives at Augusta when he won the Masters? Not so much. When was the last time somebody said as a compliment, "Man, you hit that just like Lee Janzen"? And yet the man has won two U.S. Opens. Even our golf vocabulary reveals this inherent bias for the gallant and lack of regard for the prudent. The steady player who keeps it in play and does the sensible things to save par is a 'grinder', a simply horrible label. It's one of the ultimate put-downs in Johnny Miller's lexicon and we, in our slavish desire to imitate our betters, will in turn use it to describe other players, when in actuality grinding is how almost all of us play the game.

But here's the irony: what necessitates a lot of what we call grinding are decisions made earlier in the hole that set us up for the contingencies of Plan B. We hit driver for tee shots when something shorter and with a higher loft would put us in a better position. We see windows in trees that most birds would see as safe havens in a storm. We bring an incurable optimism to situations that call for a bit of restraint.

I remember watching guests playing a particularly difficult par-four at a resort in Mexico. The fairway sloped pretty severely from right to left and the shot into the green, or what we should more accurately refer to as the second shot, required a long carry over a nasty looking waste area. Watching the preparation, execution and reaction to these second shots made me think of how these golfers would approach something like roulette. Would they stride into the casino, plunk all their chips on red 15, and then throw a little tantrum when the ball rattled into another slot? Based on the tee shots and practice swings that preceded their attempts at this shot I would have assigned comparable odds to their making it on the green on this particular hole. And yet time and again I saw all the myriad ways we golfers express surprise and disappointment on the course: the slumped shoulders, the thumped club head, the bitter shake of the head. Back at the roulette table, unless they were totally demented, I'd assume they would shrug and say "Oh well," knowing that the odds were clearly stacked against them. But golf manages to draw out the incurable optimist inside all of us and we love to let him have his shot, pun intended.

So to return to Adam Phillips' concept of the benign dictator-ship, we clearly have a tendency to let other citizens have their say. Perhaps we would be better off if we accepted that shot selection is like clothes shopping. Just because Tiger or Seve can execute a shot doesn't mean you should try it. Just because it's what everybody else is wearing doesn't mean it belongs in your wardrobe. This also points the way to a new method of evaluating our choices out on the course. Just as every husband or boyfriend has been asked "Does this make me look fat?" outside the fitting rooms of a department store, perhaps we should ask our playing partners more often if attempting a particular shot makes us look stupid. At least it would give us all a chance to be honest for once.

HOOKED ON GOLF

There is yet another psychological aspect to the game: it's addictive potential. People talk about getting hooked on the game. If you think about it, there's a certain amount of truth to this. For people who don't play with their spouses, it's something that takes them away from their families, and if they start playing during the week there's the risk that it could interfere with work. It can be a fairly expensive habit. Ever notice that often, as soon as a golfer finishes a round, he starts making arrangements for doing it again? Listen, denial is more than a river in Africa, my friends. There's still time for you to get your act together and avoid being on the receiving end of the following intervention:

"Hey, I'm glad you could make it. Listen, I'll get right to the point. We're all here for two reasons. First, and most importantly, we love you. And second, we think you need to admit that you have a golfing problem.

"Listen man, we're not laying any judgment on you. You know there's a lot of research that shows that what you have is like a disease.

There's nothing to be ashamed of. We just don't want to see you go on hurting yourself. Maybe you can't remember, or maybe you don't want to remember, but dude, you should hear the stuff you say when you're golfing. Even if you've only had a couple holes you start calling yourself stupid and curse yourself out. I mean, like you hardly ever swear, but as soon as you start golfing you're cussing like a sailor. By the time you're on your tenth hole you're wondering out loud why you keep doing the same things over and over again. By the end of the round you're questioning your senses, your intelligence, everything. We hate seeing you beat yourself up so much and we keep hoping that you'll see what's going on and stop doing this, but it's like you black out or something, and there you are the very next weekend doing it all over again.

"Look, I'm just trying to open your eyes for you man. I mean check it out. Look at your equipment. It used to be that you were happy with a two-piece ball, but now look at yourself. It's got to be a three-piece ball. What's next? Four pieces? Five? Where does it stop? And think about your driver. Don't get me started on how big it's gotten. That just freaks me out. But think about it: one thing just leads to another. Now you can't use the same size tees you used to. You need those big ones. What's next? Tees the size of railroad spikes?

"All I remember is that when you started playing you used a driver that was actually made of wood. Then it was metal, and then that wasn't enough of a thrill so it was on to titanium. Can't you see a pattern here? Are you going to be moving on to plutonium? Would you actually carry something radioactive in your bag if you thought it would give you twenty more yards off the tee? Hey, you know, on second thought, don't even answer that question. I don't think I want to hear the answer.

"Did you ever stop to think about who you're spending most of your leisure time with? That's right, other golfers. You think they're your friends, but do you think for one minute that they'd spend time with you every Saturday morning if you stopped playing? Of course not, and don't kid yourself. Yeah, yeah, they call you 'pardsie' and stuff like that but they just want you to golf so you'll start betting with them and we both know how that ends up. If you quit today, they'd forget about you until the next member-guest and then they'd invite you just so they could suck you back into their depraved lifestyle.

"I know this is going to tick you off but we hacked into your email account and frankly we were shocked. Do you realize how much of your time is spent setting up opportunities to hang out with other golfers? You almost manage to make it sound healthy and recreational: 'Got a game Saturday?' Give me a break.

"And these charity tournaments, do you really think any of us are fooled? Honestly, man, could you really tell me the difference between muscular dystrophy and multiple sclerosis? You think playing at these things makes your habit kind of noble or something? You just go because you want to play the courses and get some 'free' shirts. And speaking of clothes, when was the last time you left the house on a weekend morning and you weren't wearing a polo shirt with a logo on it? What happened to your self-respect? I'm only saying this because I love you and it hurts to see you like this.

"Look it's going to be tough, but we're here for you. Nobody gets started on this stuff alone, but nobody gets out alone either. Listen, I know this dude who kicked this thing entirely. He was like you. He grew up in a family where both parents golfed pretty heavily and he just assumed that golfing was what you did to relax and have fun with your friends. I think his parents were just like yours. They pushed it on him. They paid for lessons and got him started pretty young. It's sick isn't it?

"Anyway this guy checked into a treatment center and then joined a support group. These days he rides a mountain bike for exercise and goes ballroom dancing with his wife. Doesn't watch even a single hole of the Majors. He's completely clean.

"So we're here to help you, my friend. But I got to tell you one thing, we're not going to be fooled if you act like you're going along with this and suggest a visit to the Betty Ford Clinic. How stupid do you think we are? We know how many golf courses there are around Rancho Mirage."

CHAPTER 17

GOLF AND A
BETTER YOU

So we have wound up here, confronting this question: can golf make you a better person? Now you could pose the question slightly differently by turning it up a notch and asking if being a better golfer could make you a better person. It used to be that answering this in the negative would have entailed some sort of snarky reference to a low digit handicapper you knew who was a real douche bag. But after the Thanksgiving weekend of 2009, you need only mention one name, Tiger Woods, and the case (if it were ever in question) is closed. And sadly, and just as obviously, the converse question, whether being a better person would make you a better golfer, is equally untrue, although the aforementioned Mr. Woods advanced just that point in his Tiger 2.0 public relations campaign in late 2010. Were it otherwise, the author of these words and you, for having displayed such good taste and judgment in choosing to read them, would both be much better golfers than I suspect we are.

But to return to Tiger for a moment, I think it is difficult for non-golfers to appreciate the degree to which his fall from grace undermined a notion shared to a certain degree by all golfers: the belief that the game does instill values and habits that shape personal development in a positive way. This line of reasoning is familiar to anybody who's seen a commercial for the First Tee program that introduces inner-city kids to the game. In these ads, golf puts itself up on the pedestal as an activity that teaches among other things, perseverance, courtesy and honesty. The pitch is that golf can make these kids, or anybody for that matter, better people. Our willingness to buy into the image that Tiger's handlers foisted on us was made possible in part because we as golfers believe in the virtues of the game.

Now I want to go on record as saying that the First Tee program is wonderful and nothing I'm about to say should be construed as questioning their efforts. But the question before us is whether golf can make you a better person and if so, how. I'm not denying that golf, or any other activity that requires a great deal of practice to acquire any degree of mastery, can instill good habits that can contribute to success in life in general. But golf is hardly unique in that regard. In fact I've always felt if I had to hire based solely on a demonstrated appetite for hard work and delayed gratification I would recruit from Ivy League crew teams: "I'll take the kid with good board scores who signed up to be a galley slave." And there is of course a chicken or the egg aspect to all of this: does golf instill these values or does the game attract people who already have these innate traits?

However, one way in which golf does distinguish itself among other sports is the self-enforcement of rules infractions. But, still, I happen to believe that golf throws its collective shoulder out patting itself on the back for this feature of the game. It is certainly laudable and does distinguish golf from sports where millions can witness a violation and the perpetrator never steps forward to admit his guilt. Among the most notorious examples of this would be Diego Maradona's handball in the World Cup in 1986. But the infraction doesn't have to be as blatant as using your hand to propel the ball into the net in the biggest soccer tournament in the world. Most sports involve action where competitors try to see exactly how far they can get away with certain illegal acts. Think of the grabbing and pushing that goes on to gain position for a rebound in an NBA game, or the liberal definition of legal blocking techniques employed by the offensive linemen of any NFL team.

But one doesn't have to be excessively cynical to wonder how many infractions on the golf course go unreported, and in a game as solitary as golf, who else is going to make the call? It could be argued that golf is simply making a virtue out of necessity. Things will have to continue this way until we can start using those CIA piloted drones to supervise player behavior.

But the point remains that somebody could be an honorable golfer and call a penalty on himself and still cheat on his taxes or his wife. And therein lies the weakness in the argument that golf will make you a better person: it's all based on the idea that what happens on the golf course is transferable to the rest of your life. But the reality is that the golf course, for better or worse, is like Vegas and not only because it is also a locale for gambling: what happens on the golf course has a way of staying on the golf course.

GOLF AS A TEACHER

Certainly the idea that golf has instructive potential is hardly limited to First Tee ads or promotional spots for the USGA. It was, after all, the inspiration behind one of the most ill-timed magazine cover stories ever, "10 Tips Obama Can Take From Tiger" in the January 2010 edition of *Golf Digest*. In case you may have forgotten, or were somehow not paying attention, this edition hit the newsstands about the time Tiger was checking into a sex addiction recovery center in Mississippi. As with most efforts of this kind the *Golf Digest* story took the approach of instructing by way of analogy: match play is like a debate, big policy issues are like the majors. And that's all well and good but all of this, from the First Tee ads to the Obama/Tiger essay, misses some of the real ways golf can instruct us. And I want to be clear that I think there's more to be learned from the game than just the dour, sort of Calvinist view that the random misfortunes of your golf ball teach you how to react to all of life's good and bad bounces. I think we can get more from the game than just an admonition to sack up and stop whining, or encouragement to work hard and tell the truth.

I don't mean to minimize the importance of instilling personal virtue but life requires more than good habits. It demands that you see things clearly, that you diagnose accurately and that you ask the right questions. The tendency is to look for prescriptive lessons from golf: behave in life as you should on the course and good things will happen. In fact it can feel like there is only one degree of separation between an aspect of the game and some homily about life. An example of this is a book I found in a used book store titled, *The Front Nine-Nine Fundamentals of Golf That Will Improve Your Marriage*. It's a slim volume with a lot of pictures either of golf situations or happy loving couples doing things like walking on the beach or buying produce together. The beach thing I get, the produce buying seems a little odd, frankly. The magic moments for my wife and me have never involved finding that perfect bunch of Swiss chard. The chapters have titles like "Avoid the Hazards" (I think that's self explanatory) or "Loosen the Grip." It's more than a little corny, but the advice is still sound if blatantly obvious.

But this use of the game to prescribe behavior ignores golf's potential as a diagnostic or illustrative tool that helps us look at our lives in a different way. Golf holds special keys to helping us do those things not simply because of the way we play but the 'how' and the 'where' of that play as well.

More than any other sport the ritual and rhythm of playing golf mimics what we do in our work lives. Think about it. I am going to assume that most of you reading this are no longer hunter-gatherers, so that putting bread on the table does not depend on your foot speed, agility, ability to throw something accurately or any other skill you might possess that's useful when it comes to outsmarting various mammals or vertebrates that you fancy gutting and consuming. So what does work involve? Well, at the most basic functional level, it is a sequence of actions in which you are presented with a task, you decide on what you want to do, you execute on that plan, and then depending on outcome and temperament you either complain or feel satisfied, and if you want to, you can always analyze the result with your colleagues before moving on to the next task. For their part your audience will act like they're listening but their minds will really be on what they have to do next. And then it's their turn. Lather, rinse, repeat.

Sound familiar? Of course it does. That's what makes golf such a great lens on the rest of our lives; it shares the same structure. Tri-athletes can brag about the demands of their sport: swim, bike and run. But we golfers are tri-athletes as well: plan, execute, regret. So given this similarity between life in general and our sport in particular, what lessons are to be learned and what questions does this pose for us? Here are two of them. And please don't expect anything too subtle here. I'm basically playing with a lump of Analogy Play Dough. What we can make of all this is going to be basic and fundamental, not intricate and sophisticated, but that doesn't make the conclusions any less true.

THE GOLF COURSE OF LIFE

When talking or thinking about the game of golf we have a tendency to focus on one thing: what the ball does. Oh, look, the ball did what we wanted it to! See how happy we are. See the little fist pumps and the white guy high fives. But then, oh no: the ball didn't do what we wanted. See how sad we are. See us sulk and swear. Listen to us afterwards, when we've had a couple scotches, as we pontificate about how the random bounces of that little ball teach us about life.

Hey, I've got an idea.

Forget the freaking ball.

So now what does that leave us? Well, we've got our golf clothes, our clubs and the course itself. You can keep your clothes; there's no reason for you to get naked for this discussion. But forget the clubs. What use are they if you don't have a ball? So what are you left with? That's right: the course.

One of the interesting things about the literature about golf and life is that there is rarely a mention of what the course itself has to teach us. If it is mentioned at all it is only as the setting for those random events and bounces that can determine our score. Viewed in this way the course is no different than a board game like Chutes and Ladders: land here and good stuff will happen, but land over there and you're not so lucky. And yet there are some very interesting lessons right under our spikes. Just as scientists in the 17th century could not discern the molecular structure of matter, we golfers have not seen that the structure of the golf course is a way to organize the rest of our lives.

Consider for a moment the layout of most courses. The vagaries of topography or the designer's whims may result in slight variations but generally a par 72 course consists of two sets of nine holes, each with five par-fours and two par-threes and two par-fives. The sequence will vary from course to course, but like another great art form, the sonnet, the golf course has rules governing its structure. It has a mix of different challenges, from the short to the longer term, from relatively easy to almost impossibly challenging.

But stop and think about that for a minute. Life itself is a variety of tasks and challenges, so maybe we should step back and consider what the three types of golf hole symbolize in terms of the rest of our lives:

Par-threes: these are the straightforward tasks, the low hanging fruit that should be easy to check off the list. There isn't a great amount of strategy or planning involved. These are the one or two-step tasks, the errands and routine tasks of the day. But at the same time these are the basics that cannot be ignored: the bills, the grocery store, the dry cleaners. A life compromised of just these tasks would be boring and repetitive. This is the life that drives some suburban housewives crazy. Think of the par-three courses you may have played: no matter how great the design you still miss the feeling of hitting all those tee shots and longer irons that are part of playing a real golf course.

Par-fours: these are the challenging tasks of the day, the stuff that is giving you a little more trouble. On many courses the number one handicap is a longish par-four and for most players a good course will have some holes where par is simply not a likely outcome. Your objective in that situation is simply to give it your best and hope that you can salvage bogey. In other words you are going to screw it up somehow, or to put it more charitably, you will tend to complete the task at hand in a manner that is less than perfect. Viewed in this context, par-fours, of which there are always more than any other type of hole, are all the messy things in your life: your relationships, your vices, your neuroses. In general this is the stuff, good or bad, that never gets checked off the to-do list. It's there everyday and it's what keeps therapists and drug dealers well paid.

Par-fives: finally, the big projects, the multi-step assignments that you have to approach in stages. This is for many of us symbolic of our work lives, the realm of the project, the big presentation. But the way that we approach a par-five is also the way that many of us have to play our most challenging par-fours, with a multi-phase approach that is our way of acknowledging that we aren't going to resolve this issue quickly.

But as with a round of golf things in life are not always as they seem. A simple par-three can morph into an aggravating adventure. Think of the home repair project that looks like a quick fix and then turns into three trips to Home Depot and ends with a call to somebody off craigslist. The par-fours are the situations where it is best if you start out with realistic expectations, or in other words, you have to admit that you aren't really going to get it right, you're just going to give it your best. And the par-fives? Well let the journey begin! A bad start can always be remedied and an auspicious beginning can come to a disappointing end.

But there is a diagnostic element to this notion of the golf course as an extended analogy to the rest of your life. Everybody talks about wanting to have work-life balance but I think there's a bit more to that than being able to leave work early so you can see your kid's soccer game. And besides, I have news for you. In the brave new world of the wireless device, work is winning. That little smart phone of yours? It's never too far away is it? Sure you can leave the office but that just means that work seeps into the rest of your life through that little screen. It's not like you're Don Draper and can just put on your overcoat and fedora and waltz out the door into the unknown.

But finding balance in your life should cut a little deeper than just dividing up your hours between the pursuit of income and the use of that income. And this is where the idea of the golf course as diagnostic tool comes in. For example, imagine a life that is all par-threes: short, repeatable tasks where the objective is right in front of you all the time. This has no doubt seemed pretty appealing to all of us at some particularly stressed out point in our lives: just give me a menu of low-hanging fruit or a to-do list of mindless tasks. But the drudgery of facing the routine and repeatable would drive us crazy after a while. We may think it's a pithy way of answering the question of how we're doing, but nobody really wants to live a life that is the same shit, different day.

Or, to continue, turn up the turmoil and volume and imagine a life that is all par-fours. Yow! Personal issues, money trouble, relationship meltdowns, adolescent children. Sure, there will be stuff that you can handle but this is basically a smorgasbord of all your personal challenges. Have a nice round.

And then finally, a life of all par-fives, or the life of the absent-minded professor: Mismatched socks, lint all over the tweed jacket, yet another forgotten birthday or anniversary. You're just immersed in the project, the grant proposal or the design of the experiment. You can't be bothered to get organized, not when you've got to finish the next chapter of your book. Everything else is just background noise, and that includes not just your wardrobe but your family as well.

Now alternatively we could imagine a life that excluded one of the three types of hole, or the bad combination platters if you will. These also teach us that a balanced life requires that you do what a golf course asks of you: take on all the challenges.

Threes and fours: This is the realm of strollers and book groups, the place where you find the young mothers who anguish over whether to go back to work. It's all personal development and the dry cleaners. But there's no involvement in a bigger longer-term effort that transcends the day-to-day and provides a welcome distraction from the Big Issues that hang over you.

Threes and fives: The club for all the Type A personalities. It's all about getting it done, from the trivial to the substantial, at home and at work. Just get out of their way, and as for personal issues, that stuff is for loser crybabies.

Fours and fives: This is the most exclusive club, reserved for self-actualized big hitters who see a therapist, close the big deals and devote themselves only to the most important stuff on the agenda. On the other hand there is no connection to the activities that make all of that possible: no errands, no chores, no relationship with food aside from seeing it appear in front of you and then eating it. It might be great but it seems sort of groundless and detached. There's a big risk of becoming like George H. W. Bush and being impressed by a check out scanner at a supermarket because you've never had to buy anything for yourself. After all, there is a certain residual level of tedium in life. It's just the nature of things. For example, you can leave the corporate world behind but then you are just exchanging the torture of meetings for the aggravation of changing your own toner cartridges and the boring chore of making up your own invoices.

So, viewed in this way, the golf course itself is telling us some things and also offering a way for us to examine our lives. First, balance in your life means having a mix of all three types of challenge and so the question to ask yourself is what kind of course are you playing? A balanced life isn't simply one where you have time for work, family and recreation; that's a well-allocated life, not necessarily a well-balanced one. In order to have balance you have to have the right mix of tasks and problems, otherwise, to cite the example of life at the extremes, you can either be mired in drudgery or disconnected from the world around you. Think of it as an existential version of the food pyramid that nutritionists use to define a healthy diet. It isn't just a question of portion size; you have to be sure that you're getting the right mix of nutrients, or in this case, activities.

The next obvious point of self-assessment is to ask yourself whether you're avoiding any of the different holes in your life. Neglecting any of them because you don't like them is clearly no recipe for success, and yet there we are in that supposedly more challenging and important realm of existence that we call real life ducking and dodging certain things. You could never do that on a golf course but there we are skipping certain activities or willfully ignoring a room full of elephants. In this regard the ratio of holes in a conventional par-72 golf course is particularly instructive: the routine and the longer-term projects are less than half the holes. Over half the course, five-ninths to be exact, are par-fours, your personal challenges. The fact that there are ten par-fours on a standard course is best understood as representing the sum of the following equation: the seven deadly sins plus sex, drugs and rock 'n' roll. In other words, the ten par-fours symbolize everything that has ever gotten anybody in trouble, ever.

This is yet another example of the eternal wisdom of the game of golf, because that is how we should allocate our time and effort when we're off the course as well. Just to really belabor the analogy, when all is said and done and they're adding up The Big Scorecard, the major determinant of how you did will be how you handled the personal stuff, the issues that get messy at times and require more energy sometimes than we care to invest. Imagine being somebody who took care of business but completely blew off all the people in his life and never owned up to his own issues. There'll be a lot of flowers at the funeral but not a lot of heart in the eulogies.

But we need to avoid being too smug about obvious examples of imbalance. They can come in more benign forms. In my case I lost the responsibility for paying bills in our household a long time ago in large part because I've never been that good at the Real Life par-threes. As an inveterate procrastinator prone to dreamy distraction I had a habit of putting off the task, laboring in part under the irrational and false assumption that any time you put off paying money you were saving money. Obviously such an approach failed to factor such things as interest rates and late fees and my wife moved in to fill the breech. I'd also have to admit from personal experience that slovenliness is what happens when you aren't respecting the shortest par-threes in your life, like hanging up your clothes or putting things back in their place after using them. Being messy and the additional time that costs you just plants the seeds for double bogeys down the road. Played the right way the routines of daily life look like this: you take out a utensil or tool, use it and then put it back where you found it. But if you're a slob like me you can't be bothered with that final step of putting something back where it belongs. As a result next time you have the additional task of recreating your previous steps, finding the object you need and then tackling a chore that is now heavily spiced with a lot of swearing and fussing. There you have it: an instant double bogey.

This leads us to the final question: are we playing these different holes in our lives the right way? Or, can we apply what we've learned on the golf course to the rest of our existence? Of course we can. (I mean, did you think I was going to step away from an opportunity to beat this analogy further into the ground?) As we've already mentioned, the way we average golfers approach a difficult par-four is exactly how we should deal with any difficult issue in our lives. It is now a project, something that requires planning and best anticipated and executed as a series of smaller steps. For example, quitting smoking or controlling your diet or drinking isn't one big battle but a series of little battles. And as for the bigger tasks, the projects in our lives, we need to be sure that we approach them patiently and deliberately. At the beginning it feels like there is a lot of real estate between you and your objective but that doesn't necessarily mean that you have to try to bite off as big a chunk as you can right off the bat. The objective of each step isn't to maximize distance but to position you for success on the next phase of the process.

THE UNIVERSALITY OF HANDICAPS

Golfers take a certain justifiable pride in the handicap system. But having developed it, we tend to take a narrow view of handicaps. We see them either as a form of comparison ("Whoa, his is so much smaller than mine, I feel inadequate.") or as a subject for negotiation (Okay, alright, I'll give you two strokes a side, now stop whining!"). At the beginning of a round it is the basis for an exchange that, at the round's conclusion, is converted into something of value: money, beer, bragging rights.

And as with anything else in life, there is the half-full or the half-empty perspective on the subject, and I've noticed a tendency among golfers to favor the latter which sees one's handicap as the difference, or if you prefer, the chasm, between your predicted performance and par; in other words the difference between your game and how the game is supposed to be played. In fact you could argue that the vernacular's appropriation of the word 'par' is just further evidence of a massive conspiracy to undermine our already fragile golf egos. After all, when the word 'par' comes up in conversation away from the course and detached from any connection to the game that gave us the term, it doesn't mean great or even very good. It stands for okay or at expectation. But for the vast majority of us golfers the notion of actually shooting par for 18 holes is nothing but fantasy. We will always fall short of that mark.

But there is a half-full view as well and that incorporates not only an appreciation of how your "number" is calculated, but it leads to the realization that handicaps play a role in all of your life, not just on the course.

Remember that your index is calculated based on the following formula: first, a handicap differential is computed for each score by taking your adjusted score (that's the number that you put into the computer that uses the maximum score you are allowed to record for any given hole and not the simply atrocious actual number of strokes it really took you) subtracting from that the course rating (the score a scratch golfer would record on said layout) multiplying that by 113 (the slope rating for an average course) and then finally dividing that by the slope rating of the course you just played. In the second step you derive your handicap index by taking 96% (don't ask) of the average of the ten lowest, or best, of your handicap differentials. Voila! You now have a golfing identity.

So, as a number your index represents a reasonable and hopefully honest approximation of neither your average nor your absolute best, but rather your better game. And it is a standard of performance based not on expectation but actual data. It is important to remember that this handicap version of you is not some idealized version of yourself. It's not the doctor your mother wanted you to become and it's not the version of yourself that stars in your favorite fantasies (and not just because this version is clothed, not naked). Rather it's made out of real stuff. But therein lies the beauty of it. What you expect of yourself, and just as importantly what others expect of you, should be based on what you've done. In this way it is a welcome departure from the affirmation that I believe is the cause of so much unnecessary suffering: the notion, so popular particularly in this country, that you can do anything you set your mind to. Bullshit.

Now it is generally true that if you shoot your index you should drive home with a larger amount of money in your wallet than when you arrived, unless of course a certain somebody in your foursome manages to shoot yet another net score in red numbers. Thus, in a sense, your real opponent, or more accurately your relevant standard of comparison is not the other golfer, but this better version of yourself.

But once you realize this you start to see that this comparison between "How I'm Doing" with "What I've Been" or "What I Could Be" occurs in all our different roles in life, and sadly, explains a lot of our difficulties. Many a marriage founders when one spouse remembers the svelte version of their partner who walked down the aisle. You weren't hired because your employer thought you'd win every sale or every case, but there was certainly an expectation that you'd get some of them. They looked into the future and saw a productive new member of the team, not the sluggish version that shows up on Monday morning or the one that can't stay awake during late afternoon staff meetings. Do a good job for a client and do you think they will expect anything less the next time around? The problem with people who know you isn't just that they know your faults, but that they also know how good you can be and therefore can tell when you've fallen short of that mark.

Actually dogs provide the perfect counter example to support the notion that handicaps are a universal phenomenon in our lives. They don't have a standard of performance in mind. Just show up and they are absolutely ecstatic to see you. In fact the absence of any handicap in the canine-human relationship is one of the great appeals of dog ownership. As the bumper sticker puts it, "God, please make me the person my dog thinks I am."

With children it's a little more complicated and the sometimes painful process of growing up is marked by the shadow of the handicap version that both sides, parent and child, use to evaluate the other. When kids are really young parents can get that canine like unquestioning affection. But certainly by adolescence that starts to fade. Now, both parent and child go through a period of disillusionment. The parent suffers in comparison to the infallible all-knowing adult that the teen remembers knowing as a young child, while the parent looks at an awkwardly maturing adolescent and wistfully recalls the smaller cuter version that wasn't such a huge pain in the ass.

So, if you step back from the game of golf and look at your whole life you can see that you have as many indices, or if you prefer, handicaps, as you have roles. There is this better version of you that others are using to judge your performance at home, at work, everywhere. They proliferate like credit cards in your wallet. Now you may grumble that your spouse has you playing at too low a number, but there you go.

But now that we can see the universality of handicaps, how does being a golfer help us with this? Well, first off let's all relax and realize that the first and most important lesson is that you don't have to be perfect to be a winner. Perfection is not attainable, or certainly not over the long or immediate run. There are eagles and aces out there to be had, the flashes of the improbably accurate, but nobody has shot 54 in competition on a real par-72 course. We don't have to do that or even come remotely close to that in order to come out ahead. As mentioned above, it's the guy who shoots his index who gets paid in the grillroom after the round. That's all it takes. Just be the person you've been when you were on your game. You can do it, and you know why? That's right: because you've done it already.

But this leads to another implication, namely that you can't play to a handicap that somebody assigns to you. If you find yourself constantly falling short of the expectation that others have set for you then you aren't playing to the right standard. You may not have the right job, or the right spouse. We all have a comfort zone but that has to be defined by our actual performance, not somebody's expectation. And in the end the most important handicap is the one that you have for yourself. Only you know if you're telling the truth when you say you tried your best.

Which leads in turn to this additional piece of guidance: it's important to remember that when things get tougher, performance, on an absolute scale, tends to suffer. Scores go up; people don't behave as well. But our first impulse is often to expect just the opposite: in our hour of need we look for perfection or at least something better than the status quo, when in actuality we should be accepting that when the going gets tough what passes as 'good' is actually going to be a little worse if measured on an absolute scale. It bears pointing out that this is not introducing some mushy relativist moral scheme in which you cut everybody some slack. Remember that golf has a very strict and almost Byzantine set of rules. The idea is to distinguish between outcomes and conduct: nobody gets a free pass to break the rules; it's just that everybody gets the benefit of being judged for their effort and not the result. And the first person that you should make the beneficiary of this sort of benevolence is yourself.

CHAPTER 18

THE DRIVE
HOME

If I make all the traffic lights the drive home from my club, Lake Merced Golf Club, takes about ten minutes. I take a left on to Junipero Serra Boulevard which then immediately crosses over Interstate 280 just a mile or so north from where a sign along the shoulder announces somewhat presumptuously that this is the World's Most Beautiful Freeway. Don't get me wrong: it's a nice stretch of road but I just think there are some other worthy contenders for that title and as far as I know this issue was never put to a vote. My route then takes me past a funeral home and a relatively new theatre and dining complex called Century Plaza that is notable for the diversity of people who mill about the fountain area in front of the ticket windows. Like any of the other public commercial spaces in the immediate vicinity such as Stonestown Galleria or the Serramonte Shopping Center, this is a gathering spot for people of every ethnicity and race that can be found around the Pacific Rim. Late on a weekend afternoon it can look like everybody sent a delegation: Chinese, Japanese, Korean, African American, Mexican, Filipino, Thai, Samoan, Malay, even white folks like myself. This almost extravagant diversity of humanity is one of the things that I like best about living in the San Francisco Bay Area.

After working my way through the congestion around the theater and the adjoining parking structure I get on the aforementioned I-280 for a brief spell. This isn't the stretch that claims title to any beauty crown. Instead it arcs through the sections of southern San Francisco that are terra incognita for tourists, residents of other parts of the Bay Area and even a significant percentage of people who live in the City itself. The elevated tracks of BART, the Bay Area Rapid Transit system, run along the freeway, just to my right. The neighborhoods of Ocean View, Sunnyside and the Excelsior cover the hills to the north and south in a cheek to jowl undulation of houses and rooflines.

I take the San Jose Avenue exit off 280 and after about half a mile I come to the intersection where I veer to the left on Dolores Street, one of the great streets of San Francisco. It's a rollercoaster that runs up and down the ridge of hills that overlooks the Mission District, San Francisco's version of Brooklyn, a formerly Irish and Italian neighborhood that became the city's barrio and is now the place for hipsters and the hottest new restaurants. Dolores has a grassy median planted with large Canary palms, a tropical touch that can feel slightly preposterous on a brisk August afternoon when the wind is roaring down off the eastern slopes of Twin Peaks and the air has a decidedly Patagonian chill to it. The architecture is now predominantly Victorian and I roll up and down the hills, bay windows and brightly painted ornate facades on either side of me. At some point I take a left and meander through the grid of streets that define my neighborhood, Noe Valley. The one remaining unknown in my brief and pleasant commute is the number of couples pushing strollers who will be crossing Noe at 24th when I get to that intersection.

But at the same time something else is going on during the short duration of this drive: I'm reviewing my round. And just as my route home is essentially the same every time, this review process follows a predictable outline. Although my first impulse is to jump immediately to Areas for Improvement, in a concession to better mental health, I start with my nominee for shot of the day. Sometimes the choice is obvious: a tee shot on a par-three that left only a short putt for birdie, a startlingly accurate iron into the green on one of our harder par-fours, or a flop shot when I was short-sided that enabled me to save par. Other times I have to go with something a shade more subtle, perhaps the shot that righted the ship or the putt that inspired confidence on the greens for the remainder of the round. Sometimes the selection is more difficult simply because there isn't that much to nominate; these are the days when the candidates include recovery shots from the trees. But I can assure you of one thing: this part of the review never takes too long. If you go back to my description of the drive home I've handed out the trophy by the time I'm driving by the movie theatre.

Now I can move on the main event: going over the shots I screwed up. I don't get too carried away. I'm only interested in fingering the suspects who led my score away from the low 80's range that is the neighborhood where you'll find me when I'm playing my better game. In general it seems like there are never fewer than two a side and hardly ever more than four. If the number of bad shots on any nine holes is over four I generally give up with the review and hit, or try to hit, the mental delete button. That's too much even for me to slog through. Now the type of shot that winds up on this list and the reasons for these mishaps are hardly ever the same from round to round. That would be too easy. If that were the case then fixing the problem would be relatively straightforward. Badness in my golf game is like a low- pressure system that meanders across the entire landscape causing havoc and damage in a variety of ways.

At this stage of the book it shouldn't come as any surprise to the reader that I am not the sort who can treat a just completed round like his golf shoes, something that is simply put away and forgotten until the next time I play. Imagining what that would be like is for me like visualizing that I'm Mexican or German: I've met people from those places but I can't really see being one of them. Yet here I am playing a sport that feasts like a hungry jackal on precisely the sort of fragile mental constitution that I possess. I suppose that in the ultimate Nanny State there would be counselors whose job would be to advise young children and their parents on the selection of an appropriate recreational pursuit. I can easily visualize how such a session would go for me with the counselor tapping his pencil on my remarkably high scores for remorse and self-doubt, and yet pausing as he leaned back in chair to commend me for my equally high marks for determination and capacity for practice. "Why not take up cycling?" he would suggest, adding, "It would give you such a great aerobic workout and a chance to really ruminate."

But no, I live in the Land of the Free and the Home of the Frustrated and I have taken as my partner, in sickness and in health, in good times and in bad, this sport of golf. And so it is that eventually, after replaying the what-ifs and deconstructing what I presume to be the mechanical causes of my screw-ups, I always return to the same precepts. Because buried beneath what seems at first to be a problem with tempo or course management are always the same lessons: I should have relaxed more, I should have been kinder to myself, I should have realized in the heat of the moment that the shot at hand was one I had pulled off in the past.

But as I get older what haunts me is that I don't want to look back as I'm taking that Last Big Drive Home and think the same thing about my life. So I might as well start practicing now. Just start letting go of everything right now. Let go of the bad wedge on number seven. Let go of the club head. Let go of knowing what the score is. Just simply relax. Don't beat myself up. The game is practically screaming these simple lessons to me and yet do I pay any attention? Nope, only until it's over. I don't want to have the same set of such straightforward – and yet so apparently so easy to ignore – instructions be what I'm thinking about as the darkness closes in.

Early on in my life I came to believe that worry was a way to control outcomes, and such a belief wasn't without supporting evidence. If I worried about a particular situation or problem I was more likely to do something about it. But this was only harnessing worry as a motivator; lurking beneath the surface was a bit of magical thinking that held out hope that my anxiety could extend its tentacles over the horizon and actually influence the future. Obviously, in the end, worry can't control outcomes. Instead it only allows outcomes to control me. If I start fretting about screwing up all I'm doing is giving that unwanted result a larger set of chips to wager with when the roulette wheel that is my golf swing starts in motion. What I should be focused on is the immediate task at hand and not my reflex to anticipate what will follow right after that.

Life doesn't have a reset button and the only replay functionality we have is memory and it can feel like life has been moving forward at a frighteningly rapid pace when we do look backward. But at the same time, both life and golf give you fresh chances at the same stuff every day. We may not reincarnate but the circumstances of our day-to-day lives do. What seems repetitious or tedious about life, the recurrence, the sameness, is actually one of its greatest treasures. It's like a bucket of mulligans at your front door every day. And the challenge in almost all of these situations is not to do anything dramatic or special, but simply to do the routine task as well as you can. What we admire in the greatest players in their ability to perform under pressure: the bunker shot to save par and win the title, the slippery ten-footer to win the Open, the perfect approach shot as the whole golf world watches. Yet what we are really admiring is the ability to strip the particular circumstance of all its emotional intensity and passion and see it instead as a replay of something the champion player has done countless times before. And for the rest of us, while there may be heroic or quasi-heroic moments in our own lives, for the most part our greatness will come from the same source: doing what's normal but under special circumstances.

All the mental difficulties of the game stem from this one fact: it requires us to walk a tightrope. It calls for confidence but never to the point of the indifference that comes from taking something for granted. It requires that you know your limits but at the same time it offers endless opportunities to push or expand on those. It demands that you pay attention but it allows you to play your best only when you stop thinking.

The game is crafty in its layers of deception. Although its conventions for scoring tie all the myriad events of a round together into a number, the secret to playing the best is not having a narrative that joins every shot together. In this respect the game sets a trap for us by taking advantage of our love of narrative: our minds are wired in such a way that we make up stories and we look to find the connections between things. But as we have all learned there is no better way to screw up a good round than to tell yourself that you're on your way to shooting some special number and there is absolutely no way out of the tank once you start using the disappointment of the previous shot as a predictor of the next.

But the contradictions of the game are not all dangerous. A round can take the good part of day, unlike many other forms of recreation. Yet it is a game that you can play for your whole life. Yes it takes time to play eighteen holes, but being a golfer means you have a sport that you can play long after you've thrown your last pass or shot your last basket. If you are one of those fortunate enough to live into your eighties you too can be one of the old guys that rest of us view with a mixture of envy, dread and impatience. Yes it chews up time but golf gives years of extended life to the little kid in you who loved going out and playing with his friends. In this respect golf is like an athletic 401(k) or IRA: you put away something now so that you can enjoy it later on. Sure you can play basketball or soccer with your kids when you're young but at some point that's no longer a viable alternative. How much better if you can amble out on the course and play this game instead. Even if you're super competitive you can still do the Great Santini thing and show junior just who is the boss on the basketball court while you're still in good enough condition. However, eventually that's going to come to an end. But, if you take up golf you can still torment the young whippersnapper with a good short game and the handful of strokes you make him or her give you.

It is this opportunity for intergenerational play and competition that is one of the best features of the game. And as Tom Watson demonstrated at The Open in 2009, even at the elite level where there is no exchange of strokes to even things out, youth does not automatically have the upper hand. But for many of us the generational span of the game extends backward as well as forward. One day, long ago, somebody put a club in our hands, placed a ball on the ground and said, "Now go ahead and hit it." For us the game is not merely something we give to our children but a gift that we in turn received from our elders. We are just part of a long chain of people who have been golfers and have carried on the game. And like any inheritance or legacy this is something to be cherished and protected. The course is but a stage on which we play our small parts and we need to behave like good houseguests: follow the rules, clean up after ourselves and know when it's time to leave.

But there is an intra-generational aspect to the game's magic and therein lies yet another apparent paradox. For while the actions that comprise a round are very solitary, after all even the chattiest member of a foursome knows to keep quiet and leave you alone with your thoughts on your every shot, the game is very social. As discussed above, the action, if you can call it that, takes all of three minutes in a round that lasts four hours. The rest is just hanging out together.

That's not to say that there isn't something special about being out on a course alone in the late afternoon when there is a cathedral like quality to the light as the sun slants through the trees. But still the best times are the ones when you're out with your buddies. I mean how good can a round be if you can't get some of their money? Those of us fortunate enough to have a regular foursome are indeed lucky, and sadly, it would appear, part of a dwindling minority. When I take inventory of my non-golfing friends I find that most of them have few friends outside of work and family. They're hardly misanthropes; they're generally a pretty friendly bunch. It's just that their chosen forms of recreation tend to emphasize efficiency and aerobic conditioning and thus are somewhat solitary. We golfers on the other hand have managed to preserve that magic feeling you had as a kid knowing that you had a bunch of friends that you could join for a game. If having the time and place to still do that is a luxury in this day and age then I am indeed a lucky man.

It is a marvel this game. It will break your heart and it will seduce you. It will vex and it will exhilarate. It teaches you and it plays tricks on you. It diverts and distracts and yet it casts an uncompromising lens on the state of mind that you bring to everything in your life. It's a shame more people don't play. If you play, don't be a quitter and if you don't, how do you know what you're missing? I encourage you all to get out there, but with one caveat: don't ask for a tee time when I want one.

ABOUT THE AUTHOR

Paul Staley lives in San Francisco, where he and his wife Cathie raised three great sons. In addition to writing about golf, Paul is a frequent contributor to the *Perspectives* segment on KQED-FM. His golf blog can be found at http://whywegolf.wordpress.com. He is a member of Lake Merced Golf Club, Daly City, California. This is his first book.